I FIGHT, YOU FIGHT

ALEX NOBLE

I FIGHT, YOU FIGHT

Life isn't about the hand you're dealt... but how you choose to play it

SIMON & SCHUSTER

London · New York · Sydney · Toronto · New Delhi

I FIGHT, YOU FIGHT
First published in Australia in 2024 by
Simon & Schuster (Australia) Pty Limited
Suite 19A, Level 1, Building C, 450 Miller Street, Cammeray, NSW 2062

10 9 8 7 6 5 4 3 2 1

Simon & Schuster: Celebrating 100 Years of Publishing in 2024.
Sydney New York London Toronto New Delhi
Visit our website at www.simonandschuster.com.au

© Alex Noble 2024

All rights reserved. No part of this publication may be reproduced, stored in a retrieval system, or transmitted in any form or by any means, electronic, mechanical, photocopying, recording or otherwise, without prior permission of the publisher.

A catalogue record for this book is available from the National Library of Australia

ISBN: 9781761420818

Cover design: George Saad
Cover image: Supplied by the author
Typeset by Midland Typesetters, Australia
Printed and bound in Australia by Griffin Press

The paper this book is printed on is certified against the Forest Stewardship Council® Standards. Griffin Press holds chain of custody certification SCS-COC-001185. FSC® promotes environmentally responsible, socially beneficial and economically viable management of the world's forests.

CONTENTS

Foreword	By Kylie Gillies	vii
Prologue		xiii
Chapter 1	Who I Was	1
Chapter 2	The Accident	15
Chapter 3	In Mum's Words	27
Chapter 4	I Fight, You Fight	41
Chapter 5	In Dad's Words	49
Chapter 6	Watching the Clock	59
Chapter 7	Not Going It Alone	71
Chapter 8	In Zac's Words	87
Chapter 9	The Road to Recovery	99
Chapter 10	In Tess's Words	125
Chapter 11	Going Home	137

Chapter 12 Gratitude   153

Chapter 13 Adaptation   173

Chapter 14 Acceptance   183

Chapter 15 Vulnerability   191

Chapter 16 Discipline   213

Chapter 17 Working It All Out   229

Chapter 18 The Noble Way   247

Acknowledgements   265

About the Author   271

FOREWORD
BY KYLIE GILLIES

When Alex asked me to write the foreword for his book I was honoured, but also a little daunted. What could I possibly add to this remarkable story? I was given a manuscript that I printed out at Channel 7 where I work, holding the pages together with a bulldog clip. I carried it around in my handbag for two weeks. I even took it to Europe. And back. Without reading it. I was worried it would make me sad. How wrong I was.

I've been witness to Alex's story since the beginning. Way before he was the 'I Fight, You Fight' boy. The talented kid who got injured in the rugby accident. But once I started devouring those dog-eared pages, I could not put them down. When I finished, I messaged Alex immediately: 'Can I pop around?'

(we live in the same suburb). A text message wasn't enough. I needed to look him in the eyes and tell him how proud of him I was.

A few hours later I saw Alex, and I was slightly teary when I said to him, 'I'm 56 years old. How is it you've been able to teach me so much about life, Alex? You're only 21.'

He beamed. 'Kylie, if that's how you feel, then I'm happy. That's exactly the reaction I was hoping for.'

I've known Alex and the Noble family since 2008. Our eldest son Gus started in the same class as Alex in kindergarten. Alex was always a standout. Blond, athletic, popular. Always the first one picked for a team event. If life was a Hollywood movie, he would have been cast as the star quarterback. You get the picture. But as you'll discover here, Alex is very self-aware of just how good he had it. Until he didn't.

The Nobles were – and still are – a beautiful family. A close-knit family with three talented and boisterous sons, everyone in our neighbourhood knew them. I struck up a friendship with Alex's mum and dad, and even when our sons went in different directions for high school, the parent group remained tight. Which is how I found out about Alex's rugby accident. One second that would change his and his family's lives forever.

It was Monday 22 October 2018 and our mutual friend Susie rang me. She wanted to pop around. It was lunchtime and I was home after hosting *The Morning Show*. Something in her voice worried me. When I opened my front door, I knew it was bad. She said 'It's Alex. He's been injured in a rugby tackle. He's in Intensive Care . . .' She didn't need to say any more. It was like a punch in the chest. 'Not Alex,' I whispered. That bright, young, talented champion.

Fast forward five years.

Bright. Young. Talented. Determined. All the qualities that made Alex a champion in the sporting arena have brought him to *this* moment, this book. Through adversity, Alex has found a way to triumph. And he will inspire you to do the same.

How is it possible that what seems like the very worst thing that could happen to someone sends them down a path in life that is truly remarkable? Alex poses that question here, and the answer is almost unbelievable.

Alex had to learn to breathe again, to cough, to swallow. But somehow he finished high school, aced his HSC, and now he studies business and law at university, delivers inspirational keynote speeches, and runs a boat charter business – and the list goes on. What the . . .?

That doesn't just 'happen'. It requires a certain mindset, incredible discipline, and dogged determination. But Alex also knows how to enjoy the good things in life. When he travelled to Europe in 2022 for the first time in a wheelchair, he posted a short clip to Instagram celebrating an incredible summer with friends. I've seen a lot of videos in my time as a TV journalist, but hand-on-heart, Alex's Insta video was the *best* I've ever seen! A celebration of a young man's spirit. I cried happy tears.

Will you cry reading this book? Yes. His mum Kylie's chapter will break your heart. As a mum of two boys, I almost couldn't bear it. And to hear his dad Glen say 'I had to stand tall when my son couldn't' – it's more than any parent should have to endure. Alex's brothers Zac and Benji are a joy. This is a very strong band of brothers. And it had to be, because while this physical injury happened to Alex, the emotional impact on the entire Noble family was almost unfathomable. That kind of devastation can tear families apart. But not this one.

Alex says he often gets asked, 'If you could go back to who you were before the accident, would you?'

Do you reckon you know the answer? His response will surprise you.

Alex's has brought his story to life with the expert guidance of journalist Erin Bouda. Her natural curiosity, empathy and passion for story-telling have jogged Alex's memory of events that he would probably rather forget but wanted his readers to hear. I'm so proud of her work with Alex on this book – having known her since the day she was born, I couldn't think of anyone better than Erin to work alongside Alex to get his incredible message down on paper. Her dad Simon and my husband Tony have been journalist friends for four decades. We hold our friends tightly in our circles.

I FIGHT, YOU FIGHT

So tightly, in fact, that I remember in the weeks and months after Alex's accident our group of friends told Glen and Kylie, 'We're here for you. We're not going anywhere. Ever.' And we haven't. There are gatherings for birthdays, for 'First Friday of the Month' catch-ups, weekends away to the Southern Highlands and Mudgee.

I would often mention to Kylie how astounding Alex's progress was. She would always reply 'It's all Alex.' After reading this book I know this wasn't Mum-bragging.

I mean, I thought I knew Alex. After all, he'd been in my life since he was five years old. But I had no idea quite how extraordinary he was. He's had to grow up fast, and even the briefest conversation with Alex will reveal that he is wise beyond his years. His outlook on life? Alex will tell you that 'Things turn out for the best, for the people who make the best of how things turn out.' Think about that for a moment.

Through adversity, Alex has devised a four-stage method for achieving your goals in life. Call it a handbook for getting your sh*t together! My words, not Alex's. I read the book with a highlighter in hand. And I know I will gift it to my sons and others with one too, because Alex's messages about mastering your mind, acceptance, resilience and growth are important. And they may just change your life.

Because you might *think* you know his story. You might *think* you know the Alex Noble who was tackled in a rugby game, landed badly and spent 270 days in hospital and rehab.

ALEX NOBLE

You might *think* you know the boy who said, 'If I fight, you fight.'

But that wasn't the end.

It was just the beginning.

From left to right: Gus Gillies, Archie Gillies, Kylie Gillies and Alex Noble.

PROLOGUE

One of our family friends, who has turned into a long-term night-time carer, Stacey, once said to me, 'If only you could bottle up your mindset and share it with people, it would be invaluable.'

And when it comes down to it, that is my intention with this book.

This isn't a take-pity-on-me memoir, and I'm not a medical miracle either. I'm just a twenty-one-year-old guy who, at the age of sixteen, had an accident that changed the course of my life.

Today, I am a C4/5 quadriplegic who has done the work. I live a happier, more accomplished, more prosperous and more fulfilled life than I would ever have thought possible.

Prior to my accident, I had absolutely everything going for me and yet I was so often sad, angry and dissatisfied with my life. Since becoming a quadriplegic, I have lost so much of what I once had. But although you might find it hard to believe, I'm so much happier and more content than I ever was before. And so, I've come to realise that the quality of our lives isn't really determined by what or how much we have. It's about how we perceive it all – it's about the quality of our thoughts.

I didn't write this book because I wanted to share my story (although you'll find that here too – and let me tell you, it's a real rollercoaster ride of tragedies and triumphs!). I didn't write it because I wanted people to feel sorry for me, or give me a pat on the back. I wrote this book because I wanted to encapsulate and share the tools and tactics that have helped me control the quality of my thoughts, enabling me to survive my darkest days and enjoy the brightest moments of life.

There wasn't a precise moment when I worked all of this out – it has been a long time coming – over five years in fact. But it all started when I was recovering in ICU from my injury, and I managed to utter my first words since the accident: 'I fight, you fight.' My cousins, who were running an Instagram on my behalf and tracking my recovery, amassed 30,000 followers almost overnight after posting those words. I couldn't work out why. I struggled to understand why so many people began following me and my journey. At first,

I FIGHT, YOU FIGHT

I thought they just wanted to show their support, that they felt sorry for the poor injured kid. But after a while, seeing the messages pour in from strangers across the country made something click for me. It hit me that my words, my thoughts and my approach to life, had meaning. I was impacting the lives of others and inspiring others. Soon, 'I fight, you fight' became more than just words. It became a war cry that banded me, my family and friends, my community, and complete strangers together.

During my time in hospital, I made a decision about the way I wanted to live my life from this point forward. Every morning when I wake up, I still choose this way. And I will keep choosing it.

I've (cheekily) named it The Noble Way.

I remember when my friend Tess first told me I had a unique perspective and an important story to tell the world. I wasn't totally convinced at first, but here I am. This book is a collection of memories and stories from a time in my life that has shaped me, peppered with some of the lessons I have learned along the way, which now make up The Noble Way – four principles that have helped me not only to get through the many challenges I have faced in my life, but to grow and achieve more than I ever thought possible.

Whether you're a teenager just like I was, or a parent, a grandparent, a student, an athlete, a businessperson or even someone who is in a similar situation to me, I hope that this book can do the same for you. No matter what path you find yourself on in life, I hope it can help you to not give up, to overcome challenges, to find happiness, to be resilient, to achieve the goals you're pursuing and to be the very best that you can be.

I'm not a guru, and I don't have all the answers. I'm just a guy who's playing the hand he's been dealt and is refusing to leave the table.

If I fight, you can fight too.

Let's go.

CHAPTER 1
WHO I WAS

*'We never know the worth of water
until the well runs dry.'*
– Thomas Fuller

Remember that game you used to play at lunchtime in primary school? Where there were two captains and they each got to pick a team, player by player? You hear plenty of horror stories about kids being traumatised for life because they were always picked last.

Well, this isn't one of those stories.

I was always picked first ... if I wasn't made captain myself.

This is a story about the kid who was always picked first, who then lost his ability to play at all. But the mere fact that I was always picked first is important to this story because in order to understand the gravity of what happened to me, it's vital to understand who I was before it happened.

In a nutshell, I had everything a sixteen-year-old kid could want. A solid, healthy and loving family. A large group of awesome mates. Parents who loved each other. I lived in a nice, big, comfortable, safe home. I went to one of the best schools in Sydney, if not the whole of New South Wales. I was a good-looking, healthy, fit kid who was good at pretty much every sport I ever tried — especially footy.

When I say footy, I mean touch footy, rugby union, rugby league, you name it. I was an athletic kid; dedicated to the sport from day one. In fact, the first word I ever said was 'ball'.

Growing up, I was the middle child, with my brothers, Zac, two years older than me, and Benji, three years below. As kids, it was Zac's job as the eldest child to remind me of my place as the middle child, and it was my job as the middle child to remind Benji he was the youngest. Zac would push me around, and I'd push Benji around. And that's how it played out for fifteen years. For fifteen years Zac would fight me, push me, dominate me and beat me. But the way I looked at it was he was coaching me, training me, strengthening me, and improving me. But by the time my sixteenth birthday came around, I was finally ready to match the master. Seemingly overnight, I became the tallest, heaviest, strongest and quickest of the Noble brothers (sorry, boys) and I could take either of them on in any sport – and my God it got on Zac's nerves.

I used to play Zac in ping-pong in the garage and would beat him round after round in the first to twenty-one points. The more games I won, the angrier Zac would get and the more he would want to beat me in the next game. To be fair, I was definitely stirring the pot. One day, after I won my fifth game in a row, amid a lot of stirring, Zac's anger reached boiling point. I could tell he was going to go off, so I turned and legged it out of there – but before I'd got very far, I heard the racket whiz past my head! It smacked straight into one of Mum's pot plants, cracking it right in half. If his aim had been better, that crack could have been in my skull. But I guess if his aim were better, he would have won in the first place and there would be no need for racket throwing. All jokes aside, minutes later, we were laughing about it – best mates again. As competitive as we were, even when we fought we always forgave each other pretty much instantly.

We never agreed on much as brothers before my accident, and – as our little ping-pong tournament suggests – we generally chose to settle things 'physically'. We'd challenge each other at every turn, looking for any reason to disagree with one another and settle it by way of squaring off and punching on. It's kind of funny that 'I fight, you fight' became such a war cry for our family, because I'm pretty sure my mum didn't condone all the fighting that was going on between us before that. But, if I'm honest, it was my brothers who truly taught me how to fight in the first place. These moments bonded us, and I am forever grateful for all the blood, sweat and tears that made me who I am. The constant competition I had with my brothers shaped me, it was part of the reason I fell in love with rugby in the first place. But I like to think that what we were really doing all along was more than just scrapping – we were making ourselves stronger and more resilient for whatever challenges lay ahead. And, as it turned out, there were going to be some serious challenges to come for all of us.

While I loved all sports – sports without balls and sports with balls – I always preferred rugby. I think it was the contact aspect of it. I liked to be physical; to go hard. It's how I grew up, Zac had conditioned me for it. The ironic thing was, Mum wouldn't let us play rugby until I was about ten. It was dangerous . . . apparently. So I was signed up to play soccer instead, but my parents were eventually forced to relent to the rugby dream when my soccer coach told them I was too 'aggressive', that my tackles were too 'heavy handed'.

Then, in Year 4, when I was accepted into St Ignatius' College Riverview – a school known for its excellence in rugby – it was decided. I was signed up for the sport I'd always wanted to play, and it quickly became my whole life. I set my sights on a rugby career. And before the accident, I spent my life making inroads, and setting goals for a life as a professional player. I never had anyone telling me it was impossible. It was always something that felt achievable for me.

By the time I was sixteen, I was training with Riverview's First XV at school, I was in the New South Wales rugby sevens training squad, and I'd been selected for the New South Wales schoolboy ruby team. I often found myself playing with boys two grades above me. I was pretty okay at other sports too, and by okay I mean I was the junior swimming champion in primary school, then the senior swimming champion; I was the junior athletics champion and senior athletics champion.

I FIGHT, YOU FIGHT

Which eventually led me to Sports Captain. All right, so maybe I was a little better than okay.

It's hard to blame myself for being a pretty arrogant kid. Back then, I had a pretty sizeable superiority complex – I was stronger, taller, more popular, better looking, and a better player than many other kids my age. I was a quintessential cool kid who could get away with flunking academically because I was good at rugby. And I can say all this now, because things didn't continue that way for me, and I'm a very different person from who I was back then.

But as a teen, I considered myself as one of the trendsetters in the year. I was the typical 'jock,' lifted straight out of a Hollywood high school movie. I tried to act superior and be more mature than everyone else, going to parties at a young age and experimenting with alcohol. I even randomly convinced my entire year group that Facebook was cooler than Instagram, so everyone used Facebook. Because *I* said so. I guess it was a good thing all of my mates got around Facebook, because I remember I used to get *really* competitive about the number of birthday wishes I'd get on my wall every year. Every birthday it was the thing I looked forward to most. I wasn't even that sad when my birthday was over, because the next day was my mate Dally's birthday and I looked forward to beating his number too. I treated it like a popularity contest. I remember one year boasting that I had 110 birthday wishes on Facebook, up from 85 the previous year. I was really smug, knowing Dally wouldn't get that high a number. He didn't.

Probably thanks to all my sporting commitments, I was very competitive and also very motivated. I'd start every school day at about 5.30 am, trying to capitalise on the time I had before school to get into the gym or go to training. Ironically, that's one thing that didn't change after my accident. I still start my days early, and I still hit the gym — although for different reasons.

But back then, my motivation only extended as far as sport, and definitely not to academia. I was a mediocre student at best. I used class as an opportunity to better my game, and you would find me sitting up the back of the classroom on my phone, watching rugby highlights from the weekend that had just passed on an app called Hudl, turning to State of Origin highlight reels or motivational speeches by professional athletes once I'd run out of those to watch. I would pay attention to anything but the teacher up front.

To me, class was also simply time to recover from the footy we'd just played on the oval at recess and lunch. Most of the time I'd sit in the back right corner of the class leaning back on my chair with my hands on my head and my tie off, as many buttons undone as I could get away with, sweating nuts and dripping with water after a good dousing from the bubbler at the sound of the bell. I'd have my school bag on the ground next to me, full of textbooks that never made it out of the bag as I completely ignored whatever the teacher was talking about.

Somewhere in between all the footy, I found time to refuel, stealing the boarders' leftover food after throwing down my own huge packed lunch. After school, my fifth meal of the day was four crumpets with peanut butter and jam paired with a 'serious mass' protein shake before double training sessions for both school and rep rugby. If I only had one training session that afternoon, it would be down to the park with my brothers and mates after school instead – we'd play until Mum walked to the back of our garden and yelled over the fence that dinner was ready. I'd manage about one hour of study (the bare minimum) after dinner and be in bed by 8 pm – absolutely wrecked – and ready to do it all over again the next day.

Weekends were much the same – minus the 8 pm bedtime – but the sport was mixed in with some underage drinking at mates' houses and at parks (aka 'the movies'), whilst trying to get as many girls' phone numbers as possible. That's not a joke! I remember our first dance in Year 7 with an all-girls school called Loreto Normanhurst, where my mates and I literally set the challenge of who could get the most phone numbers. I smoked everyone with a total of forty numbers . . . I thought I was the king.

But in the same year as the school dance, I also got my first 'zero' at school. The subject was history, and the assignment was a 2,000-word research essay on the Roman Empire. We had been given two weeks to complete it, but staring at a blank Word document the night before it was due, I realised my one hour of allocated study time wasn't going to cut it. I sat there for a while trying to figure out how in the world I was going to submit this bloody assignment. A few head scratches later and I had come up with what I thought was a genius master plan. I picked up my phone and called my (smart) mate, Charlie, with a proposal that went something like, 'Hey mate, if I send you my music assignment, can you send me your history assignment?'

Two minutes later I had his essay in my inbox. A quick copy and paste job and I was done. I didn't even read it. Submitted! I closed my laptop, and I slept easy that night.

The next morning, I walked into history class with my chest out, thinking my plan was foolproof! I strutted up to our teacher, Mr McAllan, at the front of the class to say good morning, and the first words out of his mouth were, 'Alex, you've been done for plagiarism. I'm giving you a "zero" and three Saturday detentions. Good on you, mate.'

Yep, I got Charlie in trouble as well.

I didn't worry too much about the zeros I got throughout my schooling life. Instead, I spent all my time worrying about one thing. And that was how I looked; my appearance, what other people thought of me. Let me give you an idea of just how much I really cared about impressing others

I FIGHT, YOU FIGHT

while I share some of the most embarrassing moments in my life . . .

Before the accident, I used to have this wavy, sun-bleached blond hair paired with an awesome tan spread over my shredded body, thanks to spending so much time outdoors. I had this cool, surfer kind of look and I knew it. Anyway, it was around Year 9 when I remember Mum – reluctantly – taking Zac, Benji and me to Top Ryde shopping centre for haircuts. I didn't want a haircut but Mum insisted because school holidays were almost over. I sat, begrudgingly, in the hairdresser's chair and gave the hairdresser instructions like 'I like the length, I want to keep the length', and 'Please don't touch the blond on top', only for Mum to pull rank and tell the woman, 'It's all gotta go!'

And it was the worst haircut of my life. The waterworks started as soon as I stood up and looked in the mirror. I walked around Top Ryde for the next hour a blubbering mess, sulking that my crowning glory had been snatched so horribly from me.

Even earlier than that, I remember being in Year 7 when I caught the bus home from school one afternoon. I got off the bus, walked down our long, steep driveway, opened the front door and shouted out, 'Hey Mum, I'm home!' I headed down the hallway towards my bedroom and flung my backpack and sports bag across the room – one landed on the bed and the other in the middle of the floor. I turned around while loosening up my tie and undoing my top button as I began to look at myself in the mirror on my bedroom wall. Looking into the mirror that afternoon I remember beginning to pray to God and I asked him to grant me three wishes.

My first wish out of anything in the entire world was to bring Grandma back from heaven. She had recently passed away and I'd had a really good relationship with her. Grandma and Pop lived in Townsville, and loved me and my brothers more than just about anything in the world. When we visited their house, we'd run around naked on the lawn spraying each other with the hose on hot days. And even in his seventies, Pop could still do backflips into the pool and used to swim around pretending to be a saltwater crocodile coming to snap us up. Anyway, I thought that was a pretty reasonable wish – just a little more time with my grandma.

Now here is where it gets embarrassing.

For my second wish, I could have asked for anything in the entire universe. I could have wished to cure world hunger, or end world poverty, or to make the NRL – I mean, I could have even wished for the ability to fly.

But what did I wish for instead? I said, 'Lord, my second greatest wish in the whole world would be . . . to remove this freckle from my face.'

Are you kidding?! I just cringed writing that. But that shows you how much I cared about other people's perceptions of me and how I looked; how badly I wanted to impress others.

I FIGHT, YOU FIGHT

I thought long and hard about my final, remaining wish. But standing there in front of the mirror I said, 'My third and final wish . . . is to remove this *other* freckle from my face.'

Yep . . . freckles were the extent of my problems.

All I wanted in life was to be seen as the cool, sporty, good-looking, popular guy that every girl wanted and every guy wanted to be mates with.

What a purpose. What a life. If you could even call it that.

CHAPTER 2
THE ACCIDENT

'No pressure, no diamonds.'
– Thomas Carlyle

It was Sunday 21 October 2018, and rugby was the first thing on my mind when I woke up. It was also the last thing on my mind when I'd gone to bed the night before – I'd always lay my kit out on the floor of my bedroom, so I could jump into it the second I got up. I even placed the clothes on the floor in order – shoes at the bottom, above those were my socks, then my shorts, and then my shirt. So the first thing I saw when I opened my eyes was my blue and green shirt, my New South Wales Rugby training shorts, and my white ASICS boots waiting for me like a chalk outline at a crime scene. That morning, I was trialling to be selected for the under-17 New South Wales rugby sevens team, which was a pretty big deal for me.

I woke up early as usual, about 6 am, dived into my gear, and went to check that my dad was out of bed. I was still on my L-plates, so technically I needed some adult supervision for the drive to the training session at Knox Grammar School's oval that morning, and Dad had signed up for the job.

'Dad, you ready?' I said into the darkness of my parents' bedroom. I heard a grunt and then a 'Yeah' in response. I was itching to get to the session. But first, I needed to eat. I had my ritual berry smoothie for breakfast, consisting of one banana, a bunch of frozen mixed berries, two Weet-Bix, honey, peanut butter and yoghurt – all blended up in a Blitz2Go.

Taking my smoothie with me, I met Dad out front and stuck my L-plates onto the Mazda. Dad got into the passenger seat and immediately tuned the radio to his favourite AM station. My dad is a pretty knowledgeable guy, he loves to soak up information like a sponge. But listening to the morning news was definitely not my favourite way to get pumped for a training session – I would have preferred to pump some Eminem or 50 Cent to hype me up for the day ahead, but I couldn't really argue with Dad, seeing as I was the reason he was up so early on a Sunday morning.

Dad and I didn't talk much in the car. I was so focused on rugby that it was all I had the brain space for, and it never occurred to me that I could have talked to him about it, let alone asked for advice. I thought I knew it all, that I had everything under control.

As we drove down Victoria Road it started to rain, I turned on my windscreen wipers and watched them swipe the droplets against the glass. It was a miserable day, overcast and gloomy, but nothing could dampen my excitement for the training session that lay ahead.

When we arrived at the oval, I jumped out of the car and grabbed my boots, leaving Dad behind me as I headed straight for the grandstand where I could see the other players getting strapped up. I'm ashamed to say it now, but the truth was that I didn't want to be seen with my dad. Don't get me wrong, I love my dad, but I was trialling for the Open Sevens, and most of the boys were a year or two ahead of me in school. I wanted to seem cool in front of them, grown up, and showing up with my old man wasn't exactly the look I was going for. Dad hung around for a while to watch me settle in from a safe distance before heading off.

At the grandstand, I shook hands with the other guys and got my boots on. Obvious outliers as Year 10 students in a group of predominantly Year 11 and 12 boys, my mates Tom, Hamish, Dally, Bill and I stuck together. We ran our warm-up and drills on the sidelines, keeping to ourselves, until about halfway through the session when the coach split us up for a 7v7 simulation game, full contact.

I was more than ready to show off my skills in a game. I knew the trainers would be watching us closely, seeing how we handled ourselves and deciding who would get picked. A 7v7 game was the perfect way to really put us through our paces and test our stamina – there's a lot more running involved when there are only seven players a side instead of the usual fifteen.

Twenty or so minutes into the game, our team was behind and feeling the pressure – defending hard for play after play as the other side edged closer to our try line. There was relief, finally, when one of my teammates pilfered the ball and we managed a turnover – at last, we could get on the offence. In this crucial moment, my shot at proving myself had arrived – the culmination of early mornings in the gym and late nights alone practising in the park. It was my golden opportunity to fulfil my purpose, to achieve my dream. This was my time to shine.

My teammate was on my left and we were both running towards the defence at high speed. He drew the defender and just before he got tackled, he passed me the ball, a perfect long pass. I caught it – a nice catch, two hands, straight out in front of my chest. I tucked the ball under my right arm and I looked up.

I was met by a defender from the other team. To avoid getting tackled, I chucked a goose step to get around him, which is basically a movement where you slow down and then quickly speed up again. But it was contact rugby, after all, so I stuck out my left arm to palm him off at the same time. With no way to tackle my body, the player grabbed my arm; one hand on my wrist, the other on my shoulder, and he pulled me down.

I was still running as he tugged at my arm, and the momentum sent me into a nosedive. My left cheek smashed into the hard dirt first. The momentum of the tackle carried the rest of my body over the top of my head, cracking my neck.

Instantly, everything stopped. Everything went silent.

I FIGHT, YOU FIGHT

Everything went cold. Everything went numb. I was down. I was stuck. I couldn't move. I couldn't feel a thing.

Everything I had ever worked for was mercilessly shattered. My whole world just crumbled.

And I couldn't tell you how long it took everyone to run over to me, or what anyone said or did in the seconds after I slammed into the ground. But when I opened my eyes and looked up, I saw the concerned faces of thirty-odd teammates and coaching staff gathered around. Beyond them, I could see the miserable sky and overcast weather.

People often ask me if I felt pain at that moment . . . I didn't. My body was completely numb. My world sort of froze over, everything became a blur. There was only silence. There I was, lying flat on my back in the middle of the oval, looking straight up at the grey faces of my teammates and the even greyer clouds above. One moment, I had been racing towards the try line, moving a million miles an hour, and the next, everything had just . . . stopped.

The only things that I still seemed to have control over were my eyes and my mind. And in my mind, it felt as if my arms and legs were out in front of me in the air, bent in the position I'd been in just before I hit the ground. But out of the corner of my eye I could see my arm, lying motionless beside me along the ground. It didn't make any sense.

I eyed one of the stand-by physios hovering above me. He was holding my head in position, making sure I didn't try to move, not that I could have. All I could think of was the trials for the First Fifteen tomorrow at school.

'Am I going to be sweet for trials tomorrow?' I asked him. I don't remember his answer, but I was starting to figure out that this was a bit more serious than a sprained ankle. I was really short of breath, and my whole body felt strange: numb, but also cold, like I was frozen solid. I still had the strangest sensation of my arms and legs being out in front of me, bent the way they had been the moment before my head hit the ground.

Nobody mentioned calling an ambulance, or at least, I didn't hear anything about it. It felt like I had been lying there on the oval for ages when suddenly there were paramedics by my side, injecting morphine straight into my arm. With the help of my teammates, they got me onto a stretcher and placed my arms in a crossed position on my chest, the way a body is arranged in a coffin. It was so strange, I could see that my hands were up near my chin, but it still felt to me as if they were reaching out, waiting for the impact of the fall.

~

The paramedics carried me to a waiting ambulance. My mate Bill, another Riverview boy, asked if he could ride to the hospital with me. 'I'll come and support you,' he said, climbing in to sit beside me.

I FIGHT, YOU FIGHT

Lights and sirens, whipping through red lights and traffic. The paramedics gave me a bit more morphine, the maximum dose, and things got a little foggy. I don't think Bill and I found ourselves having any deep and meaningful conversations on that ride – maybe a couple of laughs, though. It still didn't seem all that serious, somehow. When I think back on it now, I realise that Bill was just trying to distract me, talking about anything and everything except what was happening in the moment.

Credit to the paramedics, no one was really freaking out. Sure, they were cradling my head, but I was still ignorant of the situation enough to ask them if they thought I'd be okay for trials the next day. I still remember their answer: 'We'll have to wait and see.'

Meanwhile, Hamish's mum, who had stayed to watch the session, called my mum and told her I'd been in a rugby accident and was on my way to hospital. She and Dad mobilised immediately.

The ambulance arrived at Royal North Shore Hospital. I still couldn't turn my head to look around, but looking up and lying there in the back of the van, I understood we were underground, obviously making our way through an emergency entrance.

I was lifted off the stretcher and onto a trolley, everyone careful not to move my neck. And then I was hurtling down hospital corridors, looking up as the fluorescent lights sped by above me. It was like a scene from a movie, the paramedics and Bill all jogging along beside me as the trolley carried me . . . where? I had no idea where I was going, what was happening. And then I was wheeled straight into an emergency X-ray room where I found myself alone for the first time. Alone, with nothing but my thoughts. But all I really remember thinking was how cold it was in that room. I was still freezing. I could feel the cold on my limbs, despite the fact my brain could not seem to get a message to them. I was just a pair of eyes, staring up at the hospital ceiling. *Please, please can this not be happening?*

The hospital staff obviously decided pretty quickly I needed surgery, as I was wheeled out of the X-ray room and into another room for a prerequisite MRI. The MRI machine is a huge tube they feed you into, but the space inside is tight, incredibly claustrophobic. My face was a centimetre away from the top of the tube and all I could hear was the beeping of the machine as it scanned my whole body. That moment felt like an eternity where all I could do was talk to that little voice inside my head . . . *What the hell has happened to me? What is going to happen to me?*

After the relentless noise of the MRI machine and my own thoughts, I was finally wheeled out and into the next room where I caught sight of my parents. I can only imagine what they were feeling, how worried they must have been – but they didn't let it show. I was being rushed to surgery, and

I FIGHT, YOU FIGHT

we had less than thirty seconds together. What do you say to someone in thirty seconds?

What was there to say?

They told me they loved me, that everything would be okay, and that they'd be there when I got out.

And a moment later, the anaesthesia took effect and I was out cold. I wouldn't wake up again for four days.

CHAPTER 3
IN MUM'S WORDS

It's a cliché to say it's the call no parent ever wants to receive, but there's no other way to describe it. I still think about it a lot. I remember it so well. It was the day my family's life changed forever.

The night before was a Saturday night, and I had been at my thirty-year high school reunion. I remember that so well, too. School reunions are always so interesting. Catching up with old friends, and noticing how much everyone had changed without really changing at all. There were air kisses and lots of 'the boys are doing great!' conversations frozen in time. But less than twenty-four hours later, those words would have been grossly inaccurate. Thinking back on it now, it was almost like the universe was giving me a chance to acknowledge how good a life I was living in front of all my old peers – an encore of sorts.

The next morning, I was standing in the kitchen of our beloved family home in Gladesville. We had moved in when I was pregnant with Benji, our third son, and fourteen years' worth of precious memories with a bustling family full of energetic boys had been created right there in that kitchen.

I was standing by our breakfast bench, my hands busied by dishes and wiping when the phone rang.

It was Hamish's mum, Jillian. She was at the rugby sevens training – where Glen had dropped Alex about an hour ago.

'Kylie, there's been an accident,' she said.

'Who?' was all I replied.

'It's Alex.'

I froze. The phone in my hand. The words would not come.

Jillian's words, however, have replayed over in my head a thousand times since that day.

She told me she could see Alex lying on the pitch; they'd called an ambulance, suggested calmly that I should make my way over there. Details were scarce, but I knew I had to move. I gathered up my handbag and house keys and got into the car. Quick and purposeful. It wasn't my first rodeo.

Being a mum to boys who loved their sport, the hospital wasn't a foreign place to us – we'd only recently brought Zac home after his second knee reconstruction surgery. While I wasn't panicking – yet – I did have a sense of urgency. I've watched a lot of football, and I've seen a lot of head knocks. I know that when someone goes down after a tackle you always wait for them to get up. 'It's okay, they're getting back up' – the crowd collectively breathes a sigh of relief. Jillian hadn't said Alex got up.

I called Glen and told him Alex had been injured and I was on my way to Knox oval in the northern suburbs. He said he'd meet me there. It was about a twenty-five-minute drive from our place and I kicked into autopilot as I weaved in and out of Sydney's Sunday traffic.

Jillian called again.

'Hello?'

The ambulance had arrived and they were taking Alex to Westmead Children's Hospital, in the western suburbs, a long way from Knox.

I pulled the car over to regroup; change direction. *Think, Kylie, think.* A few beats later and I was aggressively pulling the car away from the curb, on the move again towards Westmead – a Mum on a mission.

My phone rang.

It was Alex's friend Bill, who was riding in the ambulance, 'Kylie, we're not going to Westmead Children's, we're going to North Shore. See you there.'

I pulled the car over, again, and found myself hunched over the steering wheel. The control I had maintained up to this point was fading. I felt a swelling in my chest, which boiled over until I let out a sound unlike anything I've heard come out of my mouth before. It was guttural 'No!' It was the first of many such deep, animalistic sounds that would leave my body over the course of the next four years.

Where the hell am I going? I just need to see my son.

Arriving at the Emergency Department at Royal North Shore Hospital, the first person I saw was Bill's dad, Rowan. I looked at him, and his face took me by surprise. There was a six-foot-to-heaven mountain of a man, always the life of the party, looking at me with a face full of torture. His eyes were swollen and his face red and crumpled. Serious bawling had been taking place. He obviously knew more than I did.

The next person I saw was Dally, Alex's kindred spirit in many ways; they were born a day apart and both driven by their passion for football. As I write this five years down the track, the bitter irony resonates as Dally is in Vancouver representing his country playing rugby 7s, the very game that was to cruelly snatch away Alex's dreams of playing football again.

Back to the scene. Dally was crying too. *What's going on?* I thought. These strong, formidable jocks had been brought to their knees. Reality started to sink in.

When Glen arrived, the hospital staff ushered us all into a private waiting room. The 7s coach and manager, who were both deeply concerned, were told to wait in there too. Still no Alex. At this point, I felt suspended, like I was holding my breath and standing somewhere out of my body. I hadn't come unstuck, not yet, but I knew this was serious.

The first piece of information came from a doctor who joined us in the waiting room and told us Alex's scans were showing evidence of a spinal cord injury. They were still waiting on some secondary results to confirm, so we had to wait a little longer too. I could tell he was choosing his words carefully.

I FIGHT, YOU FIGHT

Wait. It was all we could do. Wait.

I have no recollection of the following few hours. I know they were painful and mind-numbing. The thoughts crashing through my mind like waves; the what if's; the maybes. What seemed like an eternity must have passed before we heard from the doctor that Alex was going into surgery. Surgery that could take about nine or ten hours. The doctor said we could see him before he went under.

We walked up to where Alex was being kept, lying on one of the hospital trolley beds, covered in blankets in the corridor of the operating theatres, head cap on and prepped to go straight into surgery. His face was still Alex. He gave me a groggy smile but didn't say much. I went straight to him. *My boy. My beautiful boy.* I kissed his sweet face and caressed his cheek for only a moment; I didn't want to leave him.

'Be brave, my precious son,' I uttered under my breath as they rolled him away. At this stage I started to feel even more suspended and out of body; it was surreal.

We went back to our private room to resume the endless waiting. I got in touch with Dally's mum, Kristen. Dally was her youngest of four and I had come to admire her as a woman and a mother. She came to the hospital straight away and supported Glen and me during those harrowing hours. She suggested we go out for a walk to help pass the time. I begrudgingly agreed. The three of us stepped outside the ED. The sun was shining, the air felt fresh and clean.

It probably was a good idea to get some fresh air. Or so I thought. As we strolled aimlessly, we crossed the road and found ourselves in front of Gore Hill Oval. A football field with Sunday's matches still in play; mothers and fathers watching their sons enjoying their active lives. This was the sight that finally broke me.

My body went limp, the feeling of suspension heightened, a wave of nausea, dizziness – all the strength in my limbs left me, my body gave way and I collapsed onto the pavement. Glen and Kristen caught me, but they let me slide and put me into a comfortable position. The wind had been taken right out of my sails. I felt outside of my body. I didn't have the will or the energy to get up. Small graces; collapsing outside a hospital meant I was given immediate attention. An ambulance came out of nowhere and I recall a warm smile and a competent hand assisting me onto a stretcher and into the ambulance which brought us a whole fifty metres back to the emergency waiting room.

Over the coming weeks and months ahead, I would become familiar with the different ways that grief would involuntarily pour out of my body, leaving me in the foetal position. If my son was losing control of his body, maybe in some sick way I was too.

The next six hours or so were a blur of nausea, angst and trepidation. It was about 10 pm when they told us Alex was out of surgery and they would take us up to meet the surgeon.

I FIGHT, YOU FIGHT

I was still uneasy on my feet and unable to walk properly so I had to be helped into the surgeon's office and then into the chair at his desk for the post-surgery results. I shuffled down in the chair so my neck could be supported by the back of it; my head lolled to one side and my eyes glazed over. Glen sat a little straighter next to me. Some long-gone, logical thinking version of myself pulled out my phone to record the impending conversation in case we ever needed to refer back to it.

I still have the video. I have not once been able to bring myself to listen to it again.

'Something something something – severe spinal cord injury, Alex is unlikely to ever walk again – something something . . .'

'Ever walk again' were the only words I heard or understood. Nothing else mattered.

That's it. Never again. Alex won't walk. Never. Alex won't be able to walk ever again. That's it. Never.

Catastrophic injury.

Quadriplegic.

Wheelchair.

The words spun around and around in my head.

As an English teacher, I knew what catastrophic meant – but I'd only ever used it in the melodramatic context of 'That's a catastrophe!' In the context of this conversation, it was a literal scientific term to describe what had happened to my son.

Adjective: catastrophic.
Involving or causing sudden great damage or suffering.

I found myself hating the surgeon. I hate him.

Of all my boys – actually of every kid I knew – this couldn't be happening to a worse one, I remember thinking.

Alex was our middle child, but you wouldn't know it by how he carried himself. He was the whole package. He came into the world at 4.4 kg (a big baby), and was walking by ten months old. Even from the way my hair and nails shone when I was carrying him, I knew he was going to be impressive.

People flocked towards Alex. They were drawn to him. I'd watch him on the school playground, where he would literally have a small army of other children following him around and taking his lead. Before he got to school, I'd had to put him into pre-school early to satisfy his need for human interaction and attention. When he was old enough to understand, I remember pulling him aside and reminding him what a privilege it was to be so well liked and so good at sport . . . and to always remain humble.

All three of my boys were obsessed with sport; they bounced off the walls at home, where Glen and I were always running around after them. It was exhausting work. Every weekend we were tag-teaming to get them to their various sporting commitments – soccer, then touch football, cricket, swimming, tennis, you name it.

I FIGHT, YOU FIGHT

My eldest, Zac, and Alex were always competing with each other over one thing or another. They fought a little as a result of being so close in age, and Alex was always able to give Zac a good run for his money. Alex was skilled physically. And he had the discipline to match. We were well aware of his potential to do well in his chosen sport.

Of course it was rugby.

Once we finally let him play, that was it. Alex lived and breathed it. He would not miss a beat; would not miss a session. In the weeks leading up to this fateful day, Alex even skipped a family trip to Cairns to play rugby. Any chance to play, to progress up the ladder – he really did dream of making it to the top. He used to absolutely ride Glen and me about being on time to drop him at training; we'd be roused out the door, always arriving early.

It was dawning on me that this was never going to happen again.

Then one of the most intrusively jarring thoughts you can have as a mother popped into my head – if I know this kid, he's not going to want to continue his life like this. And that was okay, if he didn't want to, then I wouldn't either, I bargained. That's probably a hard bargain for you – the reader – to comprehend. But that was precisely how I felt. Put it down to maternal instinct. Put it down to motherly love.

Glen didn't recognise the shell of a person that I'd become by the time we walked out of the surgeon's office. But as the stronger one of us, he implored me to stay strong too. He said, 'Whatever you do, Kylie, you have to stay strong in front of him. You have to.'

I promised him I would.

Alex hadn't woken up from the surgery, and we figured we should probably get some rest too, not knowing what the next few days could bring. The hospital gave us a room with two couches, which Glen and I pushed together to make a quasi-double bed. For the next two weeks we slept in that room, scared to death and clinging to each other, night in and night out.

Word had got out among our extended family and friends about what had happened, and offers of help started flooding in. Our youngest son, Benji, was taken in by a school friend. I didn't even know the mum, Maree, from a bar of soap, but she said Benji could stay as long as we needed him to.

My own mum was around too, helping Zac, who was in the middle of his exams for the HSC, the senior high school certificate in New South Wales. Luckily, he could drive, so he was able to get around between school and home and his other commitments.

Glen and I found ourselves studying, too. Quadriplegia. It was one thing to find out your son had suffered a catastrophic spinal cord injury, but to learn everything that goes with it felt like blow after blow after blow. Things like bowel care, enemas, catheters, pressure sores and temperature control.

I FIGHT, YOU FIGHT

Then there were the thoughts a mother couldn't help but have: *How is he going to have a normal life? Is he going to fall in love and have children? Will he ever get a job and travel and do all the things normal young people do?* I know that these were, in some respects, selfish thoughts, but I couldn't help but think them. I also couldn't let my mind go there if I was going to stay strong like I had promised Glen.

Spinal cord injuries are so case-by-case – unique to each patient. The small piece of hope we clung to in the days ahead came from our clinical nurse specialist, Matt, who was a godsend and an expert in quadriplegia. He spoke to us in facts and statistics that we could understand and gave us positive, real-life examples. Matt told us about the efforts the doctors were making; how they were pumping Alex's neck full of fluid and medication in an attempt to regenerate his spinal matter. He told us that you just can't predict what type of movement any patient is going to get back. He told us it could be up to a year until we understand the full extent of the injury.

So there, in the darkest days of my life, there was still a little bit of hope. And we only needed a little.

When tragedy of this enormity strikes a family, you never know what is going to happen. But at the time of writing this, it has almost been five years since his accident and as I started to contemplate the idea that maybe Alex's life could end up greater than it was before, he came past me one night and said: 'Mum, we're all good. You're all good. You have everything you need. We have the best family in the world. Look at us.'

And perhaps he is right.

Here we all are. All living The Noble Way.

CHAPTER 4
I FIGHT, YOU FIGHT

'It's not what happens to you, but how you react to it that matters.'
– Epictetus

When I woke up four days later, the last thing I could remember was my parents telling me everything was going to be okay.

People get injured playing footy all the time, I thought. This was just another injury, right?

I was in a bed, totally unaware of where I was, what day it was, what time it was or what had happened to me. I had a split-second thought that I was just waking up in my normal body, in my normal bed at home – you know that feeling? When you're totally disorientated in those first few moments after waking up from a great nap?

But I went to turn my head and I couldn't. Went to get up, and I couldn't. Went to talk, and I couldn't.

I fell into a state of shock. I was so scared, I started freaking out. I went to scream out loud for help . . . but I couldn't even do that. I lay there with my legs, arms and head completely pinned to the bed, unable to move or make a single sound. So, I just stared straight up to the white ceiling above me. It was me and the ceiling.

It took me a while, but eventually – after the grogginess and drowsiness of waking up from a four-day coma died down a bit – in my peripheral vision, I could see wires and tubes and cords and monitors and machines everywhere. I could also hear the machines humming and beeping at the same time. They were all hooked up to my stomach, my chest, arms, hands, shoulders, neck, mouth and nose. It didn't take me much longer to realise that I was in hospital, and the only things keeping me alive were machines.

But Mum and Dad were by my side, as promised.

They had spent the past few nights sleeping (if you could call it that) in a break-out room reserved for loved ones in the hospital. The surgeon, Dr Hartin, had given them my diagnosis: I was waking up as a C4/5 quadriplegic.

There was actually never a moment (at least not one that I can remember) when anyone explained to me what had happened. There wasn't a point where I was told, 'You're a C4/5 quadriplegic, you've lost all movement in your body from your shoulders down – you'll most likely need a wheelchair for the rest of your life and never walk again.' I didn't ask questions either; I don't think I wanted to know. How definitive and depressing would the answer be? I was okay, just lying there, numbed by shock and probably lots of painkillers too.

In my privileged life up until that point, I hardly knew anything about quadriplegia. I had never known anyone with it, which in hindsight, was lucky, because it meant I was able to work out what the injury meant for me; I had no real knowledge of the limitations of a spinal cord injury, so I didn't restrict myself to them. I think my parents steered clear of having the 'quadriplegic' talk too. Knowing me, knowing it was something unproductive to say out loud.

As I would later learn, a quadriplegia diagnosis is a matter of centimetres. My trauma was on the fourth and fifth vertebrae, hence why they called it 'C4/5 quadriplegia'. A C1 quad is someone who's trauma occurs at the very top of their spine. On the cervical part of the spine (the neck part), each vertebra is numbered from C1 to C7, starting from the top, nearest to the skull. The higher the number, the lower down the spine is the injury and the more control you retain of your body. So basically, if my injury had been a centimetre higher, I would be able to do so much less, and if it were a centimetre lower, I'd be able to do so much more. But what was the point of dwelling on that?

The severity of my situation did dawn on me in the waking hours and days that followed. I realised that I was only being kept alive by machines, and that I now required assistance for every basic human function.

I was only able to breathe thanks to a huge tube down my throat, one that permanently moved my teeth into new positions. Pretty painful. I couldn't talk or drink water or eat on my own. That was the tube's job, too. When they finally said I was allowed to shower after days without one, the nurses rolled my body like a dead weight onto a special shower-bed and pushed me into a wet room.

Feeling hopeless and useless, I saw a dark path before me. A life of not being able to do things I wanted to do, to achieve the things I wanted to achieve. A life of sadness and negativity. A life of loneliness, too – because who would want to be close to someone who was nothing but a burden on others? A life as a guy sitting in a wheelchair, just waiting for time to pass. I didn't want that kind of life. I couldn't have that kind of life.

There's this book I love that sort of sums up how I approached the following days in ICU. It's called *The Boy, the Mole, the Fox and the Horse* by Charlie Mackesy. In it, a boy and a horse are walking through a forest. The boy says to the horse, 'I can't see a way through,' and the horse replies, 'Can you see the next step?' The boy says yes. And the horse tells him: 'Well, just take that one.'

Just focus on what's right in front of you, Alex.

Maybe this wasn't just a regular footy injury ... But I didn't see the point in fighting it. When a storm hits and there's absolutely nothing you can do about it, sometimes you just have to let the wind take you. Sometimes that's all you can do: hold on for dear life, ride it out, and wait for the sun to appear. And somehow I managed to take each new learning, accept it as my current reality and carry on. One challenge at a time. Looking back, maybe that's how I coped.

Fast forward through a blurry five days, and I was lying in my bed in the ICU – it was about 8 or 9 pm and dark outside.

I FIGHT, YOU FIGHT

The days were hopeless and long, but I only ever concentrated on the task or challenge that was laid out in front of me by the nurses and hospital staff. I was still unable to make a single sound on my own.

That particular night, I remember my mum, dad and my older brother Zac sitting at the end of my hospital bed. I was lying there, staring at the ceiling (still all I was able to do at that point) and they were having a conversation in the kind of whispered, hushed tones reserved for an ICU ward late at night.

The place was quiet enough for me to hear them. The topic was Zac's HSC. Zac, in the middle of his final exams, was trying to convince my parents that sitting his remaining ones would be a mistake. He had already sat the English test, but his maths exam was the next day – and he hadn't even picked up a workbook. My accident had derailed his study plans; he was distracted, and he would rather give up after everything that had happened to us as a family. He was going to throw in the towel.

Mum and Dad told him it didn't matter about the final result, that he should still see it through and finish his schooling. I agreed with them, and lying there I was awash with guilt. Silent. I knew Zac was saying all of these things because of what had happened to me – because I was injured. And this same injury was stopping me from saying the one thing I wanted to say to him the most: 'Keep going.'

So – with every single bit of strength and might I could summon – I opened my mouth, swallowed a small sip of air, and I spoke for the first time in five days.

It was a weak, whimpering sound, but the room was still enough that they could hear.

I said, 'Zac, if I fight, you fight too.'

And that's how it started. *I fight, you fight.*

We laughed at the profoundness of it all, but deep down we also knew that it was true: from that point on, we were going to fight.

CHAPTER 5
IN DAD'S WORDS

I wasn't shocked when Alex said, 'I fight, you fight.' Maybe because I already knew he was a fighter. But it was quite a surreal moment, regardless, because he had just had the breathing tube removed from his throat and could barely make a sound! No one was expecting him to speak, let alone say something so profound.

Like Alex, I didn't have the luxury of being weak in those months after the accident. I had to be strong for Kylie, our boys, and most importantly, for Alex. I was the patriarch of the family, and I found strength in finding purpose. Some of that purpose I found in becoming the unofficial official spokesperson for our family. I sent updates via WhatsApp every day for at least the first thirty days when Alex was in intensive care and at the spinal unit.

This is the first one I sent:

On Sunday morning 21, Alex was doing what he loves most. He was training with the U16 NSW Rugby 7s selection squad at Knox fields.

There was a nasty training accident, and Alex landed heavily on his head. An ambulance was called and he was taken to Royal North Shore Hospital emergency.

ALEX NOBLE

Alex was admitted immediately to ICU for a CAT scan and MRI. Alex sustained a broken C5 vertebrae, and worse, a dislocation of the spine and damage to his spinal cord. The surgery inserted metal braces between C4 & C6 from both the front and the back of the neck to stabilise and decompress the spinal cord.

Alex currently has no feeling in his extremities. However, we received some faint hope when he moved his biceps on Monday. Alex has been on a breathing ventilator since admission. However today this will be removed and Alex will be monitored to ensure he is breathing comfortably.

The extent of the damage will only be known over the next few weeks and months. Alex will likely be in ICU for about 1 week and no visitors are allowed. He will then be relocated to the spinal unit here – which has a reputation as the leading spinal unit in Australia. Alex will be there for a while, then probably go to Ryde rehab.

Kylie and I are overwhelmed by your massive love and support. We cannot possibly deal with everyone one on one, but please keep the wave of love and prayers flowing. Alex, Kylie, Zac, Benji & I all need your help. Please pray for Alex. Love The Nobles

Our family was so embedded in our local community – through sport, our neighbourhood and the boys' school – that I felt an obligation to keep those people who loved Alex so much updated on his journey. I didn't think, I just wrote. There was never a question as to whether they needed to be on this journey with us.

I FIGHT, YOU FIGHT

The support in response to those updates came in so thick and fast that I had to ask people not to reply to my messages; but we also saw an opportunity to try and channel that support somewhere, somehow. About two months after the accident, a few friends approached me about a charity event for Alex. As the average total cost of a spinal cord injury is around $10 million, we knew we would be staring down the barrel of financial trepidation and battles with insurers, so Alex could do with all the help he could get. Kylie wasn't really capable of engaging at that level yet, but with those friends' help we put on the Alex Noble Sportsman Lunch at my mate Bill's pub, The Palace. It was the first glimmer of a little fun returning. There were many, many tears, but it was also where I had my first laugh in sixty days.

Our community began to roll out ways they could help us. One game-changer was a regular Meal Train delivery of dinner to our house – a godsend since we were at Royal Rehab virtually every day. Others could help us through charity events. Alex's school put on a couple of events; Lane Cove Rugby, Wests Tigers, Rugby Australia, the Wahroonga Tigers Rugby Club and Holy Cross Rhinos all put on charity games and days. Other companies such as M.J. Bale also ran some campaigns, plus many people supported me personally in their own ways. Even my work place, Macquarie Technology Group, put on an incredible evening for our customers, suppliers and partners called 'A Noble Event'. This event helped enormously in supporting Alex. We are forever thankful to all.

Each event seemed to generate a higher profile for Alex and suddenly there was interest in Alex's story not just from people we knew and loved, but externally from the media as well. Again, I found myself being the conduit. Through school and friends we already knew Channel 7 TV personality Kylie Gillies and news journalist Robert Ovadia, who were the first ones to broadcast Alex's story. It definitely wasn't something we loved doing – putting ourselves out there made us feel so exposed and made the whole thing feel so real – but we knew it was something we had to do. Looking back I don't know how we did it, but every time I was asked to speak, I pulled myself together and tried my best to be coherent. My job was to stand tall, while my son couldn't.

I cringed during every one of those media appearances when they used the word quadriplegia. In fact, admitting to myself the extent of Alex's injury was one of the biggest challenges for me personally. For the first twelve months after the accident, I didn't use that word at all. His spinal cord injury was classified as 'incomplete', meaning the spine wasn't completely severed. There was hope in the ambiguity. It wasn't final. It was incomplete.

While throwing myself into the marketing machine that slowly became Alex's life, I also found a purpose in learning everything there was to know about the condition I couldn't yet say out loud, and the more I learned about quadriplegia, the more I seemed to learn about the various streams of hope. There were options. There was rehab, but there were also mountains of seemingly unutilised research that became an obsession for me.

Our friends Susie and John were watching TV one evening, and heard a professor talking about a neuro stimulation technology which they wanted to bring to Australia, specifically the University of Technology Sydney. They tracked the professor down and arranged a coffee meeting. Before I knew it I had taken on an unofficial role leading a small group, Friends of CNRM, including Tess (more about her later), John and Susie, and Kylie plus a couple of other supporters, in helping to arrange the funding and marketing of this facility. I even received a commendation from UTS in December 2019. Regrettably this program has since been disbanded due to COVID-19 issues. It almost became more than just about Alex – trying to make a difference in this space became about everyone in the spinal cord injury community.

Next I learned about neuroplasticity – if they can remap neurons in your brain, how come they can't in your spinal cord? Well, research shows they probably can. Why can't Alex try that? Don't get me wrong, I wasn't just clutching blindly onto hope with every research paper that came across my Google search. I'm an engineer by trade, and there is proof a lot of this technology and research can help. The problem is it's majorly underfunded.

It's hard to put into words what I would do just to get my boy onto some programs. With the help of my new friend Greg, I spoke to researchers in Switzerland (Lausanne University Hospital) and the USA (Kentucky Spinal Cord Injury Research Center), who are achieving incredible results using spinal neuro stimulation technology. An Australian organisation, Neura (Neuroscience Research Australia), is conducting world-class research programs using neuro stimulation and is currently carrying out human trials. Neura is well supported by a wonderful and passionate fund-raising organisation called Spinal Cure. We wish them rapid and mighty breakthroughs!

Another key stream of spinal cord injury research showing some promise is stem cell therapy. There is great work coming out of Griffith University in Queensland, which has an incredible funding-raising partner, the Perry Cross Spinal Research Foundation. Their research has progressed to human trials. I also have to give a special mention to Royal Rehab in Sydney, which has recently established a world-leading technology facility with a promising visionary strategy, of which Alex is currently a part! I won't stop until we know everything there is to know about living with a spinal cord injury.

The research gave me hope, and in the early stages of Alex's injury I became an advocate of this idea that he needed both rehab and research. Although results from either still seemed a million miles away, time is what we suddenly had a lot of. I remember one of Alex's exercise physiologists at Royal Rehab telling me that sportspeople can sometimes make the best spinal cord rehab patients. They set clear long-term goals. They're used to putting in the work. They lose, they get injured, they don't get selected, and still they turn up. They turn up and they train and train and train. Then, and only then, do they stumble across the little big successes.

CHAPTER 6
WATCHING THE CLOCK

'The secret of happiness, you see, is not found in seeking more, but in developing the capacity to enjoy less.'
– Socrates

Those first few weeks in the ICU I remained effectively pinned to the bed. I was a board that couldn't move. A prisoner in my own body. I was flat on my back, and the only things I was able to move on my own were my eyes.

I knew at that point that if I put my focus on all the things I couldn't control – everything I had lost – it had the potential to completely destroy me. But if all I could control were my eyes, then I was going to focus on that. What I *could* control.

I looked around the room. My eyes darted from wall to wall, up and down, as I tried to prove to myself I still had something grounding me in my own physical body. As my eyes tried to take in the room, restricted by the brace strapped around my neck, I could see a glimpse of a digital clock to the left of me. In a life that felt a million light years away, seeing the clock reminded me of always watching the time tick by in class – counting down the hours until lunch or rugby.

The hospital clock was black with red LED numbers – or at least, I thought it was. I didn't have the movement of my neck to know for sure, so I made it my first mission to be able to see it properly; to read the time. I knew if I tried hard enough, and strained for long enough, eventually I would be able to. It gave me something to work towards.

In the twenty-four hours that followed, it was just me and the clock. When I wasn't drifting in and out of drug-induced sleep, my waking hours were spent trying to find enough movement and momentum to see it. I let it occupy my whole brain. I didn't leave room for anything else going on inside my head – and that was the point.

After a full day of straining to the point that I thought my retinal arteries might burst, I finally saw it properly. I had done it. I have no idea what the time actually was, but I was too stoked to care. The day was a success. I considered it a small win.

Speaking of time, I had plenty of it in hospital, but I knew from the outset there was no way I was going to waste any in a spiral of negative thinking. I wasn't going give in to sadness and misery, or waste my one and only life. So, I armoured myself up for whatever obstacles were coming my way, and charged ahead, disregarding those emotions at all costs. I had clocks to look at; things to learn. I am often asked if I ever cried. I didn't.

I looked at it like this: I was in a situation where I had three options.

The first option was to get bogged down and ruminate about what I had 'lost' – to wish it hadn't happened to me, to think about everything that would never be the same again and feel sorry for myself. But where would that get me? A life of grief I could never escape.

I FIGHT, YOU FIGHT

The second option was to try and look forward, but that wasn't a great option either. Looking forward in the sense of trying to see the 'end game' would have derailed me. The task was too great, the future was too unknown. The big picture was scary and overwhelming.

The third option was to simply *be*, exactly as I was in the moment I found myself in, and take on challenges as they came. If you can boil down any situation to an isolated moment, you'll realise that you're probably okay. Everyone's alive, the room is not on fire, you're still breathing.

I knew that the situation I found myself in was completely uncontrollable and there was nothing I could do or say or think that could possibly change that fact, and I knew that trying to control the uncontrollable would only result in me spending all of my time grieving. I would spend my time wishing that it hadn't happened to me, complaining about how unfair it was and how unfair life is, and I would probably spend every day for the rest of my life asking the question, 'Why me?'

The thing is, when life sets us back, time will go on, no matter what. Life isn't going to wait for us, and if we don't let go of the past, we are going to spend the rest of our time reflecting on the moments in which we have suffered, feeling sorry for ourselves. We get stuck in the moment we got hurt, imprisoned by that memory, trapped in our past, while we waste the rest of our time on Earth, forgetting to live.

So, through all the pain and agony and grief, I realised I just had to accept it as soon as I could and find a way to carry on. Since then, I've found that no matter how many doors shut in front of you, no matter how many opportunities get taken away from you, new doors always open. And if you ever feel like all the doors are shut and there's nowhere else to go, sometimes you just need to take a walk down the corridor. All you need to do is actually look.

During my time in the ICU, I realised that our minds are the only things we have complete control over, the only things that are ever completely ours. In one moment I had full control over my whole body – I jumped up out of bed, I was making my smoothie, I was driving a car, I was putting my shoes on, I was running around the football field – and bam, just like that, in the blink of an eye, it was all taken from me, forever. But my mind? Nothing and no one could ever take that from me. No amount of hurt or damage or trauma could touch it. I realised the only way my mind could be taken from me is if I chose to give up.

They say radical acceptance is what stops you from turning a moment of pain into a lifetime of suffering. It means accepting the facts as they are and not having an emotional reaction to them, not playing victim to your own life. If I had let my thoughts become consumed by the negativity, I would not have had the mental clarity to face the challenges ahead of me.

I FIGHT, YOU FIGHT

So when I was tasked with learning how to breathe on my own again, there was radical acceptance despite the fear I had. On the fifth day, it was finally time to remove the breathing tube from my throat and try to take my first breath on my own. I was so scared. I tried to speak and tell the doctors that I wasn't ready, but I couldn't. I tried to shake my head, but I couldn't even do that. So, again, I used the only thing that I could, my eyes. I opened my eyes as wide as I possibly could to show the doctors that I wanted them to stop. I even moved my eyeballs from the left to the right to replicate a shake of the head, but nothing worked. Once more, I was left with only one option – to accept the challenge.

And so . . . I took the leap.

The doctors removed my breathing tube, and immediately – as a matter of life and death – transferred me to a different machine, an intensive care-grade CPAP mask. It was strapped around my whole head and face, covering my nose and mouth. The mask *pushed* air into me and *pulled* air out of me, making my lungs retract and expand without me physically having to do it. The aim of this machine was not only to keep me alive but also to train me to breathe again. When the mask pushed air in, I had to try to suck air in. When the mask pulled air out, I had to try to blow air out. So, for the next four days, it was just me, the four walls and the mask. Night-time was the worst. When no one was around, when everything went dark and silent, the repeated sound of the machine became unbearably loud, like a never-ending freight train. And the scary part of it all was that if my body wasn't moving at the exact same speed as the mask – if I was a millisecond out of time – I would lie there, choking, just me, the dark room and the mask, unable to tell anyone about it. The fear of asphyxiating from a mistimed breath and the loudness of the machine both kept me up for four whole days.

Teaching my body how to cough again was a whirlwind too. As you can imagine, not being able to move your mouth, not using it to eat or drink or breathe, and lying there with a tube stuck all the way down your throat meant that my whole oesophagus had become clogged by spit and phlegm. Twice a day, two physios came in to 'relieve' this with what they called 'cough therapy'. Another mask was put over my face, and one physio would be attached to the other end, tasked with literally sucking the cough out of my lungs while the other put pressure on my abdomen to act as my core muscles 'coughing'.

Ice chips were the first thing I was allowed to put in my mouth. I couldn't swallow water because of all the surgery that had been done on my neck, but they'd let me suck on ice so I could try to alleviate the dryness in my mouth a little.

I honestly think the worst thing about my time in the ICU was not being able to drink water. The ice cubes were just a tease. At school, I used to carry around one of those protein shakers, and after I'd finished my shake, I'd fill the shaker with water and it would double as the water bottle

I FIGHT, YOU FIGHT

I'd carry between classes. Man, I lay there fantasising about that thing, I even dreamed about the *glug, glug, glug* noise the bottle would make, imagining tipping water out of the big opening into my mouth. I would have polished off six full bottles, given the chance. When the doctors finally allowed it, my first sip of water after five days was the best thing I've ever tasted in my life. Over the coming days, ice eventually became water, and then watered-down yoghurt.

A speech pathologist was the one to slowly introduce foods into my diet again. Understanding how mouths work and what I would be able to manage swallowing, the speech pathologist started out with yoghurt, and eventually I graduated to a diet of mainly mashed up things like bananas and scrambled eggs. The pathologist would always start small, with a teaspoon of anything to make sure it didn't make me cough, because I couldn't do that on my own yet and there was a chance I'd choke.

These small achievements were what my nurse, Matt, wanted us all to focus on too. Just the next step in the right direction. Things like, 'Today we're going to take this tube out' or 'We'll have your physiotherapy schedule mapped out by the weekend, won't it be great when you can get back into the gym?' or 'Just a few more days here, and we'll move you out of ICU and up to the spinal cord unit'.

It sounds grim, but through slowly relearning these basics, and achieving these small things, I learned the power of the mind. Of my mind. If I could just control the negative perceptions, the judgements, the thoughts about how tragic it was that I couldn't actually breathe on my own, then I could control the way I reacted and how I felt about the situation. If I could do that, I'd be able to find a true sense of achievement in what I was slowly being able to do.

Controlling the judgements around my situation was a life-changing mindset I adopted in the ICU. I like to think of it like this: imagine being approached in the street by someone speaking a language you don't understand. And in their foreign language, they begin calling you names and putting you down. They're telling you you're worthless, you're hopeless, and that the world would be better off without you. Now, how are you going to feel and experience this situation? Well, you have no idea what they're saying, so you're not going to attach any judgement or meaning to it and it's not going to upset you.

Now imagine you're approached by someone speaking your own language, saying all the same horrible things. You now understand it, so you attach a negative judgement to it; you take it on board and it then makes you feel awful.

The lesson here is that it's not the actual stimulus that evokes emotion in us – the stimulus in both these examples was the same, just in different languages – it's the judgements we attach to that stimulus that make us feel a certain way. In the same way, it's not our circumstances that make us feel

I FIGHT, YOU FIGHT

good or bad or happy or sad; it's the judgements we have about those circumstances that make us feel those things.

This mindset managed to take me from focusing on how awful it was needing two physios to help me cough, to realising how lucky I was that someone was there to help me cough so I didn't have to lie there in silence choking.

We have the power to control our judgements, despite our circumstances, which means we have the power to control our emotions and how we feel about a situation.

I still work to control my thoughts by concentrating on simply accepting what happened to me and carrying on. Being present. Focusing on what I do have rather than looking back on all I once had.

Bad things are always going to come our way in life – no matter who we are or what we have – so how are any of us supposed to stay happy? As I would come to discover, the answer is pretty simple: we just have to find a way.

CHAPTER 7
NOT GOING IT ALONE

'A society grows great when people plant trees in whose shade they shall never sit.'
– Greek proverb

Deciding to fight came from deep within. It was pulled out of me by hearing Zac talk about his HSC. I realised this was a two-way street; if everyone around me is fighting for me, then I would have to fight for them too.

How could I not? I had round-the-clock doctors and nurses keeping me alive, and I had my family by my side, day in and day out. Two hundred and seventy days of hospital and rehab in the end, to be exact.

Those days in ICU were tough. I couldn't talk or move, I didn't have a clear idea of what was going on or when I'd be able to get out. And if that sounds like hell to you, well, let me tell you – it got worse. Somehow, I also had head lice. Yep, the nits found me at my lowest point and went to town on my scalp. It felt like my head was on fire! Imagine, your head is so insanely itchy it's all you can think about, and not only are you unable to scratch it, you're also unable to tell anyone to scratch it for you. Talk about torture. And it may sound strange, but I think having head lice in the ICU was actually an important life lesson for me – it was truly the first time I realised the power of someone else's helping hand. As soon as I could talk, I remember telling my grandma, 'My head! It's so itchy!' Nanna gave my head a good scratch, took a look, and confirmed the infestation. She got some lice shampoo and the nits were history. Grandmas are the best. But the people around me did so much more than just scratch my head.

At first, the only visitors I had in hospital were my immediate family – Mum, Dad, Zac and Benji. Between them, they made sure someone was by my side at all times. Eventually Nanna and Pa were allowed in; actually, I'm surprised they managed to keep my nanna out for as long as they did. She's an incredibly strong woman who's had her own struggles in life, but she never lets anything stop her. She'd march down the hospital corridors, always ten steps ahead of Pa, but always looking back over her shoulder to check on him. That's what my nanna's like – always looking out for everyone else. She was retired, so she'd come to the hospital almost every day just to sit with me so I wouldn't be bored or alone.

About a week after the accident, a few of my best mates – Connor, Zane and Jayden – paid a visit. And I guess they hadn't got the memo about my condition, because the first time they visited, they brought me my favourite foods – an Ogalo's chicken burger and chips with a chocolate freddo (the Italian iced drink, not the frog) from Dolcini's to wash it down – evidently unaware that I still couldn't get water down at that point. One of them did attempt to feed me a chip, but I choked and the boys ended up needing to call a nurse to help me get it back up. Choking aside, there was definitely something nice in knowing that nothing had changed between us. It still hasn't.

I wouldn't be who I am today without my mates. They carried me, both physically and mentally. They haven't changed the way they looked at me; they don't treat me any differently. Sometimes they still tackle me out of my chair, or try to drown me (lovingly). But they also give me my injections and pick my nose for me, and if that isn't love I don't know what is. And despite what they say, I know it's not just because hanging out with a quadriplegic helps them skip the lines at bars. No one wants quick drinks so bad that they would risk getting covered in urine on a night out while helping me go to the bathroom.

Those same friends pretty much had to take a crash course in caring for a quad, but never once did they treat it like a chore. These days, when my dinner is put down in front of me, one of them is reaching for a knife and fork to cut it up into bite-sized pieces before I even have to ask. They fix my feet if they are about to fall off the footplate of my chair, and someone always packs my jumper or scarf in case I get cold. It's a role every one of them has adopted with total pride and selflessness.

My parents didn't leave the hospital for the first two weeks, and together we really leaned in to our faith. Mum and I said a lot of prayers. She carried around a little purse with four different prayer cards and each night we picked one out to read together. She also stuck a miniature cross on a light fixture hanging above my bed that I could see in my direct line of sight. I liked that. She carried rosary beads and bottled holy water on her too.

Mum was always lending an ear, and a few times a day she would lean in close and put her cheek against mine as she whispered words of comfort only we could hear. She would check I was okay; make sure I was comfortable. A couple of times she asked me to tell her how I was feeling out of ten. I knew if I told the truth about how I felt it would break her heart. So, feeling like a one, I always said ten. My goal was to make sure Mum stayed afloat, because I knew if I caused my mum pain and suffering, it would bring me down to a cold zero.

When there wasn't anything left to say between us, Mum made sure my laptop was always ready and charged so I could watch a movie to pass the time.

One of Mum's favourite sayings is, 'The most important thing for a mother is that her sons are happy – that's all that matters', and she practised that every day, reserving her time to be upset or frustrated about the situation for when she was at home. By my side, she stayed strong for me; she was always fighting for me.

While Mum was all about making sure I was comfortable in hospital and working to get me home as quickly as possible, Dad was about the big picture – my future. Dad dealt with the insurance companies, the lawyers, he facilitated charity events and set up the I Fight, You Fight foundation after word started to get out.

Dad also created a WhatsApp group with all the important people in our lives, keeping them across any updates and news from the hospital with daily messages.

Once Zac finished his HSC exams (and didn't fail), he and his mates spent most of their days off with me in hospital and then rehab before they started uni in March the following year.

From the moment I moved up to the spinal unit at North Shore Hospital to the day I left rehab, my uncle Brian was by my side for five or six days a week, spending hours at a time in the gym with me. He's a guy who's all about fun, and that rubbed off on me. He spent countless days making sure I was okay, cracking jokes and ultimately just focusing on the goal at hand.

My friends, and even friends of friends, would often visit in groups – large groups, sometimes ten or more at a time – and after my first two weeks in hospital, I had probably had over a thousand visits. It got to the point where the nurses had to start turning people away.

While my family and friends were keeping me afloat, they were being held and supported fully by the community around us. Mum used to say it was like our family was stuck at sea – alone and cold and dark in the middle of the ocean.

But before we had a chance to worry about drowning, a boat full of people appeared from nowhere and plucked us out of the water. Our life rafts.

Things started arriving for Mum and Dad's makeshift room at the hospital – fridges and toasters and clothes. People just wanted to give and give to help us stay afloat.

A couple of weeks in, a mate's mum, Kristen, created an online roster on an app called Meal Train to manage meals they planned to cook and deliver to us. We had meals provided for us every day for at least six months. The meals were dropped at home or at the hospital, depending on our schedules, and in 270 days, I don't think I ate a single hospital dinner.

People I hardly knew were chipping in. Suddenly one of my biggest supporters was Zac's mate's mum, Antonia, who rostered herself on for multiple breakfast shifts, bringing scrambled eggs, yoghurt and fruit that she'd stay to feed me, spending a couple of hours at a time.

My cousins had heard about the first words I had spoken in hospital, and they set up an Instagram account on my behalf, amassing nearly 30,000 followers by the time I was well enough to pick up a phone and understand what that even meant.

The outpouring of support from people I didn't even know was pretty special. I remember lying in bed one night, listening to Zac by my side reading out some of the hundreds and hundreds of texts, Instagram and Facebook messages I had been sent since the news of my accident got out. There were people I looked up to, people I used to play against, people I had met once, people who I knew only through association, or who I didn't know at all, reaching out and offering words of support. The feeling of being supported and held by that many people was something that's hard to explain.

Word was spreading fast and soon it wasn't just my immediate network reaching out. I began getting messages of support from rugby greats like Cameron Smith, Billy Slater, David Pocock and Johnathan Thurston, to name a few. Cameron Smith's message was just what you'd expect from the only man to have ever played 400 NRL premier league games: 'Keep your chin up, keep fighting.' My story reached beyond the rugby community too, and one day I was shown a video message from Delta Goodrem, and then Hugh Jackman. Hugh had some pretty sage advice that's stuck with me. He said: 'Keep your spirits up and remember that you are part of a massive community that loves you, that supports you. Lean on them, this is the time to ask for help and to lean on all those people who really want to help you out.' At the time, I was still a bit hesitant to ask for help when I needed it, but when Wolverine tells you that it's okay to lean on your loved ones, well, you'd better listen.

Then there were the A-listers who didn't just send a message, but actually paid a visit – Josh Dugan, Angus Crichton,

Reece Hodge, Bryan Fletcher and even the Governor-General all made time to schedule a visit once I got to rehab. While I was there, the Wallabies invited me along for a training session. And when I arrived for the session, David Pocock was literally standing on his head. No joke, he was doing it as part of his training to strengthen his neck, but it definitely wasn't how I imagined a Wallabies practice session to go down. After I put my eyeballs back in my head, the players showed me around their new headquarters at Moore Park, so I could check out their epic gym facility and learn a bit about how they trained. The rugby community has been really supportive of me and my recovery, and it was awesome to get behind the scenes and see how NRL legends are made.

Somehow I also became an honorary member of *Love Island*. Before my accident, I'd been a big fan of the show – remember, my main interests at that time were sports and girls, and *Love Island* had a whole lot of one of those things! A friend of mine somehow got in touch with the producers of the show, and before I knew it the cast was dropping by for regular visits. I don't know what the nurses thought about Taylor Demir, Millie Fuller, Dom Thomas and Amelia Marni showing up in all their glitz and glory to visit me, but I reckon they probably thought we were up to mischief.

During my stay in the spinal cord unit, I met a guy called Harrison who had become paralysed after a car crash that happened a few days after my accident. We were actually in ICU at the same time, but we didn't cross paths until I was moved upstairs to the spinal unit after a few weeks. Harrison and I shared a room in the unit, separated only by a curtain. If you think about it, we were kind of like cellmates in prison – at first, neither of us knew what the other was in for, and we didn't speak for a while. I was lucky enough to have the side with a window, and I realised that the view from his side of the room must have been pretty boring. One night, there was a storm raging outside, and I remember the first thing I ever said to him was, 'There's lightning outside.'

After my icebreaker about the lightning, we spent weeks on our backs, metres apart, sharing yarns about rugby and school and life through the curtain that separated us – all without ever actually knowing what each other looked like. Turns out Harrison was two years older than me and we had a lot in common.

Harrison left the spinal cord unit before me and moved to the Royal Ryde Rehabilitation Centre (Royal Rehab for short). Compared to the unit, Royal Rehab was a palace – it had a barbecue area and tennis courts! So I told Harrison he'd better reserve the room next to his for me. I was planning on getting over there as soon as possible to claim it and I was next in the queue to be dispatched (there was a list of names displayed on an electronic board). But only days later I got a text from Harrison:

Some blonde chick has stolen your room, mate!

I didn't know it at the time, but that room-stealing blonde chick was going to end up playing one of the most important roles in this story. Her name is Tess.

I'd actually seen Tess at the hospital before I met her – she always seemed to be shuffling around, wearing a neck brace and looking like a bit of a zombie, to be honest. Tess was a little older than me and I was confused about why she was there – after all, she could walk! I didn't find out what had happened to her until much later, but I'll let her tell you all about that soon.

At the rehab centre, Harrison had been allocated room 17, and Tess had taken 'my room', room 19 (I've finally forgiven her). I got room 20, the next room down, and across the hall was room 18, which was occupied by a jockey called Tye. After a few months, Harrison somehow managed to snag room 1, which was about five times the size of the rest. And this made room for Ash – who had broken his neck diving off a jetty – to eventually slide into room 17, where we all parked ourselves to watch *Game of Thrones* (Ash was a massive fan). That crew would become my life raft for my stay in rehab and beyond. Seven months in neighbouring rooms meant we became pretty close friends. The paper-thin walls helped. And sometimes they didn't . . .

One night, my mate Jayden came to visit me, and we were sitting around in my room talking about a festival we were planning to attend in a few weeks. We were pretty excited, talking about all the acts we'd be seeing. I could hear Tess across the hallway having a way less exciting conversation with her doctor. Meanwhile, my mate and I were wondering if anyone would be taking MDMA at the festival – you know, when in Rome, and all that – and he asked me if I'd ever thought about trying it. I said I wasn't sure how well it would go down with my medication and condition, but I realised I didn't really know what would happen. So I did what I often do in moments of doubt: I shouted, 'Hey, Siri—' and then I asked the question, *'Can quadriplegics do MDMA?'*

Siri barely had time to answer before my phone suddenly pinged with a text. It was from Tess:

NO WAY!!!!
Siri x

As you can probably tell, Tess became our rehab group's unofficial big sister. She was always looking out for us, and because she could still walk she helped us with all those little things that suddenly become so hard to do when you're in a wheelchair: turning off the light, getting ice for a drink, picking up something you've dropped. But she helped me in more important ways too, just by being a friend. She was always up for a chat, and even got me thinking about the future and planning my life after rehab.

Just like Mum and Dad's room at the hospital, my room at Royal Rehab was a manifestation of the outpouring of support I had around me. I had been told I would spend around eight months there, so my family made a point to make it feel like a home. It was decked out with ornamental rugby boots and cards on the wall. Then there were the jerseys. Rugby clubs from all over Australia had caught wind of my injury through the media and my growing Instagram account, and I accumulated about twenty jerseys – all signed with messages of support from players I admired. I hung them proudly on the walls. Tess also gave me a Himalayan salt lamp just like the one she had in her room.

When my parents eventually arrived at the decision to sell our family home – it was five split levels and had way too many stairs! – those same people came together for a working bee to help us move. The move wasn't easy, particularly on my brothers, who knew selling the house we grew up in meant life was never going back to how it was. But we had each other, and the big change was made easier by all the people around us.

My whole life, I had thought that I would be considered weak if I ever asked for help. I thought I would seem soft if I ever told someone I was struggling. I thought I wouldn't be a man if I asked for support because I was out of my depth in a situation. So, I kept it all in, I bottled up all my emotions and I tried to take on the world by myself. But that was before

I FIGHT, YOU FIGHT

I found myself in a situation I couldn't possibly get through on my own.

I still hate the constant need to ask for help – I need help opening doors, getting food, leaving the house, going to the bathroom, you name it. But what my family, friends and community have shown me is that asking for help does not actually make you soft or weak. Instead, it gives you the ability to get up and carry on, even when you may not have the strength to do it on your own.

While I know I'm often unable to return the favour physically, I hope I am helping them in other ways. I hope my actions, my message and my existence inspires others to keep fighting.

CHAPTER 8
IN ZAC'S WORDS

The first thing you need to know about Alex is that he's disciplined and he likes to win.

It wasn't always easy growing up with a little brother who just won't quit until he wins – who knows what he wants, and how to get it. One of my earliest memories of Alex is of him riding away on my trike. It was a pretty sweet ride, bright red with yellow wheels, so no wonder Alex – even as tiny as he was back then – was always trying to take it for a spin. He obsessed over that trike for so long that eventually my parents gave in and got him one of his own.

Pretty soon, though, just riding around on his brand-new set of wheels wasn't enough for Alex. He wanted a real racetrack to prove himself on. So, what's a big brother to do? I got some permanent markers, and together we drew a racetrack . . . all over the pavers in the backyard. We were absolutely stoked about it, zooming around all the hairpin turns we'd created. Mum and Dad were less than impressed. They made us scrub it off as best we could. These days I run my own pressure-cleaning business – I could erase that track in ten minutes without breaking a sweat – but back then it was all elbow grease!

As we grew up, Alex got more and more laser-focused on his sport. We'd play touch footy in the backyard, and he really took to it. But the most impressive thing about him even back then was his discipline. He'd want to keep going until he'd done ten perfect plays in a row, because that was how Cooper Cronk from Melbourne Storm trained. And when I wasn't around to throw the ball at him, he'd do it himself: passing it at a metal pole and catching the rebound over and over. I mean, you've got to admire that level of determination.

We were super competitive, always playing against each other, always revving each other up. Even though Alex was two years younger than me, he was an incredible sportsman. You wouldn't have caught me saying it at the time but in some things he probably had the upper hand, despite the age gap. I'll never forget the day he finally beat me at ping-pong – I'm still salty about it. I may have been a bit of a sore loser – I was always getting geed up when Alex scored a try or beat me at something – but Alex? He was a bad winner. He'd run straight to Mum, bragging about his victory. 'I beat Zac! I beat Zac!' Absolutely unbearable!

Our youngest brother Benji took the heat off me and Alex a bit. I used to get them to wrestle each other, stirring Alex up by saying I thought Benji was tougher. 'I'd bet on Benji,' I'd say, just to watch Alex squirm. My words must have had power, though, because one time I remember little eleven-year-old Benji actually picking up a fifteen-year-old Alex and tackling him right into a gyprock wall. Benji is a bit shorter

I FIGHT, YOU FIGHT

than lanky Alex, but he makes up for the height difference with strength — and the dent in the wall was there for evidence long after Alex's bruised ego recovered. These days, Benji plays rugby for the Australian Barbarians and, in my completely unbiased opinion, he's one of their best players. I reckon Alex and I get some of the credit for that — all the wrestling we did as kids paid off.

We were totally ruthless, always going at a hundred per cent. I remember once Alex and I were at a soccer camp on the Colo River, just west of Sydney, and we thought it would be a great idea to throw rocks at each other. We were total idiots, hiding behind boulders and pegging rocks as hard as we could without a second's thought. I spotted the perfect piece of ammunition — a decent sized rock, just out of reach — and decided to sprint for it. But before I even got to it, a perfectly aimed missile hit me right in the forehead, leaving a bloody gash. I guess all that passing practice paid off too.

It wasn't all crash-tackling and throwing rocks. We laughed a *lot* growing up. And to this day, once Alex and I start laughing, we can't stop. Benji and I are pretty hyperactive, always cracking jokes, and even though Alex is a bit more of a thinker, he loves to sink to our level and laugh with us about the stupidest of things in his spare time. And once we get started laughing, we really can't help ourselves — just a look is enough to set us off in another fit.

There was a time, though, when Alex thought he was a bit too cool for us. He was a moody teenager, and he had a pretty high opinion of himself. I guess it wasn't completely unfounded – he was always a popular kid. So popular, in fact, that when I was in high school, girls in my year would come up to me and say, 'Are you Alex Noble's brother? He's so hot!' Seriously? What about me?!

Clearly, Alex being a hit with the girls really got to me, because when he was fifteen I wrote him an email with the subject line 'Why Alex Will Never Get a Girlfriend' – obviously hoping to take him down a peg, in the way only an older brother can. I was working on my essay-writing skills at the time, figuring out how to construct an argument. I think I did a decent job. 'Firstly,' I wrote to my little brother, 'you cry over everything and can't cop a hit. "Muuuuuum, Zac hit me!" This quote clearly shows Alex's lack of power over me and his incompetence to cop a hit or dish one back, which relates to him not being able to get a girlfriend, because he wouldn't be able to stand up to her.' *A solid argument*, I thought, but I didn't stop there. I trashed him for having 'weird looking hair', and then finished off with the final nail in the coffin: I claimed that Alex was selfish. '"Alex, may you please put my rubbish in the bin?" "No way." This quote shows his selfishness, which is why he will never get a girlfriend, because how will he be able to give her his love when he is too absorbed in himself?' Full marks, right?

I FIGHT, YOU FIGHT

Wrong. It was all in good fun, but I couldn't have been more wrong about Alex. I mean, for one thing, he has that amazing head of curls. Besides, my little brother has copped more in his twenty-one years than most people cop in a lifetime. And even in the worst of it all, he's never stopped looking out for others – that's the opposite of selfish.

The day Alex had his accident, I was studying for my HSC when I got a text from a friend: 'Hey, so sorry to hear about what happened to your brother.' What? I was so confused. However, given how hard Alex usually went at training, I figured he'd probably broken an arm or something. That'd be right. It didn't really hit me that something more serious could have happened until I got a call from the rugby coordinator at our school who told me Alex had been injured, and he was going to drive me over to the hospital.

When I got there, the doctors explained the situation, but I was still really shocked and confused. I asked if I could go in and see him, and they told me he couldn't have visitors just yet. It really hit me then; I finally got it. Something terrible had happened to Alex, and I couldn't even be with him. Thinking about that moment now is so painful. It was like the rug had been pulled out from under me, I was caught off balance, I didn't know what to do or think. How could anything bring down my brother, the kid with the perfect footy pass, the ping-pong champion, the guy all the girls at school had crushes on? It didn't seem real.

But there we were in the ICU, with God knows what going on behind curtains and doors. I just wanted to see him and to know that he was going to be okay.

For a while, after his surgery, Alex was completely out of it. We stayed by his side around the clock, waiting for him to wake up. I should have been studying, but it was completely impossible to concentrate. I just wanted to be with my family when Alex woke up.

I was talking about giving up on doing my exams when Alex found his voice again. 'Come on, mate, you can do it,' he said. 'If I fight, you fight.' I'll never forget those words. I don't think I realised just how powerful they were at the time, but I do now. When your brother tells you from his hospital bed to harden up and fight, you listen.

There were some heavy moments in the ICU, and we were all feeling fragile, but there were good times too. When Alex got nits and our nanna was busy combing the lice out of his hair, I asked him to show us his latest trick – moving his arms. He focused really hard for a few moments, and then his hand shot up straight into the air and smacked Nanna in the face. She was a good sport about it – we all laughed.

And it was awesome to see how much support we had around us. It was actually kind of ridiculous. The school, Alex's rugby team, his mates – there were so many people who helped out. After a while, we started to bring back the good vibes, the laughter. Alex's room was always packed with

I FIGHT, YOU FIGHT

friends and family. Sometimes it was standing room only, and we never wanted to leave.

I remember once I was there with some of our mates when the nurses said visiting hours were over. We dragged ourselves out of there and went walking down the lawn towards some trees in the hospital grounds. Suddenly, we all just went for it – snapping branches, throwing stuff around, letting off steam and letting it all out – allowing ourselves to actually feel everything we'd been trying to bottle up. We had a bit of a cry, and a hug. I think we all really needed it.

When Alex moved to the rehab centre, I'd go there every afternoon after work and join ten or twenty others. We'd mess around down at the duck pond (I won't say what we did there, because what happens at the duck pond stays at the duck pond) and sometimes we'd play basketball. We'd put a rugby ball in Alex's lap and chase him around in his power chair.

It was always a big moment whenever Alex got back some feeling or movement. I don't know if you've ever been super excited about somebody else's big toe wiggling, but I have. Because everything Alex has achieved has been hard won. Instead of letting himself get frustrated over the things he can't do, he just keeps fighting – he keeps doing the things he *can* do, over and over again, just like when he was throwing the footy at the pole – until he reaches his goal and sets a new one. It takes so much strength, mental and physical, to do what he does every day, just to keep himself fit and healthy so that when new treatments are available, he'll be ready for them.

Alex is certainly not that little kid who went crying to Mum anymore. He's got a lot going on upstairs – he always thinks about everything carefully – even if he doesn't always share it. He never just says something for the sake of it, but when he does speak, he always asks the best questions. That's how you know he cares. He'll listen to every word you say, ask some really wise and insightful question about whatever you were rambling about, and as you answer he'll give you this little Alex nod of approval.

Whatever my email essay might have argued, Alex is one of the most grateful and humble people you'll meet. He has an amazing positive influence on those around him; I've seen how people in our friendship group have changed for the better, just from knowing him and watching him fight. As a family, we've gotten a lot closer too – sure, we still have arguments about the portions of food on the table, but I think we're all pretty grateful to have each other. Alex has changed me, too. There was a time, about a year after his accident, when I went off the rails a bit. I don't think I had really processed what had happened and how our lives, and Alex's life, had changed. When I get sad or angry I tend to take it out physically at the gym, but Alex has shown me how important strength of mind is for healing. He taught me to hold myself accountable.

I FIGHT, YOU FIGHT

How proud am I of Alex out of ten? Two hundred and thirty-six out of ten, that's how proud I am. And I know that's not great maths – Alex is the one who's good with numbers – but it's true. A lot of people are inspired by sports stars and celebrities, and there's nothing wrong with that, but I can't really think of many people who are more inspiring than my little brother.

And the million-dollar question: will Alex ever get a girlfriend? Well, she'd have to be a pretty special person to get *my* nod of approval. Because Alex has a lot to offer beyond his chat head. He's intelligent, highly motivated and so, *so* tough – tough enough to be somebody's rock. And underneath that, he's got to be one of the most compassionate people on the planet: he really cares about people, and he listens. Alex has a pretty special way of looking at the world, really thinking deeply about things, and he's wise beyond his years. How many twenty-one-year-olds can offer all that? Maybe I should write his Tinder bio. I think I could make a much better case now than I did in that email, anyway.

Alex has a bright future ahead of him. He still likes to win. I know he's not going to stop fighting for what he wants – he'll go the whole way with whatever he sets his mind to. I'd bet my whole heart on it.

CHAPTER 9

THE ROAD TO RECOVERY

'He who has a why to live for can bear almost any how.'
– Friedrich Nietzsche

It's well known that the period immediately after an injury is a small window in which you have to maximise your chances at reclaiming as much movement as possible. Medical specialists explained to me that the sooner I got back into it – into moving and retraining my body – the better my recovery would be. In simple terms, move it or lose it.

So hitting physio as hard as I could was my next goal. I wasn't feeling sorry for myself, I had radically accepted what had happened to me, I had controlled my judgements of the situation, and found peace being grateful for all that there was still to be grateful for.

Don't get me wrong, I knew I was staring down a long road ahead of me, and my focus definitely wasn't on big, future goals at that point. But when the process is long – and the goal is hard – it can be really easy to feel defeated. Small goals were all I was able to set myself, but I had faith that they would accumulate to a point where I could eventually set my sights on bigger things again.

I knew I had no time to waste. But I could also see how easy it would be to get stuck in a negative thought pattern: 'Why me? My life is ruined! What's the point?' I knew spiralling into that way of thinking could mean missing the window of opportunity.

I had been told I might not regain any movement from the neck down, but given my injury was incomplete, I was hopeful of reclaiming some use of my arms. I remember saying to Mum in one of those first cheek-to-cheek conversations we had while I was trapped in the ICU bed, holding onto her hand like I was holding onto hope, 'Mum, as long as I get my arms back, I think I'll be okay.'

So we started with arm exercises. Well, attempting to do arm exercises.

It was about three weeks after the accident, while I was still at Royal North Shore Hospital, that I got back into the gym for the first time. What an odd thing it is, to go to the gym when you literally can't even flex, let alone move a muscle!

I soon figured out this type of training was focused on just one muscle, a very big and important one – my brain. The idea was that through physiotherapy, I could recreate the neural pathways from my brain to my different extremities and body parts, and ultimately try to reconnect them (just when I thought the mental heavy lifting was done!).

For the first exercise, I was sitting down with my arms out in front of me held up by slings. The arm slings were there because I had no chance of moving my arms on my own against gravity. I actually had no chance of moving them on my own even when they were in the slings – my physios moved them for me. My job was to simply try to *imagine* that when my arms were making the slightest movements, that it was my brain telling them to behave that way. I say 'simply' but it was anything but simple. It dawned on me that thinking about and trying to imagine yourself flexing a muscle that you can't even feel or connect to is *way* harder than flexing a muscle the regular way. The fatigue was worse too.

I guess that's a pretty good definition of being a quadriplegic. Not a scientific one by any stretch, but becoming totally disconnected from your body means every neural pathway your brain once had in place to help you move your body was gone. Even once those pathways are re-established, you need to use them repeatedly, over and over again, for that movement to become a regular function again. Some evidence suggests it takes 10,000 repetitions of a particular behaviour to start to alter your brain chemistry. It's sort of like a baby learning how to walk; consistently trying and falling over and trying again and falling over until that neural pathway becomes a default.

Retraining my brain and body required an approach that was different to the one I was used to at the gym. As a formerly fit guy, I used to go to the gym with set goals – I might have wanted to bench press 100 kg. So I would go to the gym and I would start by bench pressing 60 kg, and every week I'd consistently add more weight until I got to 100 kg. I could see the progress unfolding in front of me, and I was motivated by that progress. The rehab gym is very different.

It was often hard to identify any progress at all, making motivation hard to come by.

'What's the point?' That question came up a lot. I was constantly asked to do things I knew I couldn't do yet, like, 'Bring your hand to your mouth . . . just squeeze, just squeeze,' and I'd say, 'I *am* squeezing!'

It's not a linear process either. Some days I'd find that movement in my arms, and other days I wouldn't. It was unpredictable. The first time I squeezed my arm on demand was actually one night lying in my hospital bed. I hadn't managed it in the gym, but as I lay there chatting away to Nanna, who had come by for a visit, my left arm shot up and nearly punched her in the face. We laughed a lot about that. That was a good moment. An extremely hopeful moment.

Next came table exercises. Physios would place a table down over my lap, and put my arms on two bits of paper on the table to help lessen the resistance when I tried to move them. I'd slide my arms a matter of centimetres on the slippery surface. After I had accomplished that, I finally graduated to what my physios called 'the hand cycle'. At first, I couldn't actually move it with my hands at all – it was automated, moving my hands for me – but it was all about working that neuroplasticity: getting my brain to realise that my arms were capable of movement; I just had to connect to them.

Here's how I thought about it all. Imagine if I put a chicken parmigiana down in front of you – one of those big boys from the pub, sitting pretty on a tower of chips, complete with salad and gravy – and I asked you to eat the whole thing in one bite. You'd tell me it's impossible.

It would be. But what's definitely *not* impossible is sitting there, cutting it up and finishing it slowly, bite by bite.

That was the approach I took in rehab, and it is still one of the most effective ways I've found to deal with any seemingly daunting task life throws at me. I cut big tasks up into smaller, much more manageable, pieces. I focus on and persistently attack those smaller bites; I don't cast my net so wide that I'm seeing the insurmountable road ahead. I set small goals that will help me reach the major goal, and I try to fall in love with the process.

You know that feeling when you are trying your very best, day in and day out, and you are still not seeing any results? When you feel like nothing ever goes your way? When you feel like asking the question *'What's the point of all this?'* It's these moments in our lives where true persistence and resilience are really needed.

I only got where I am today through taking this chicken parmigiana approach to life: from learning how to breathe, eat and drink again on my own, to the next big goal at rehab. And I haven't stopped.

Don't get me wrong; resilience only exists because difficult and dark times do. But resilience is choosing to get back up each time life knocks you down. It's the act of choosing hard work, determination and grit over giving up – even though it can be so easy to do so sometimes.

Anyone who's ever achieved anything great has met with failure. But what sets them apart is their ability to get back up and transfer a loss to a lesson.

Thomas Edison conducted thousands of failed experiments before he lit up the first light bulb.

Michael Jordan has missed over 9,000 shots, lost around 300 games, and even flunked 26 game-winning points. Yet, he is arguably the greatest basketballer of all time.

Colonel Sanders' special recipe was rejected 1009 times. But if he hadn't tried for the 1010th time, we wouldn't have KFC!

To achieve big goals, we need to attack one task at a time and refuse to give in – no matter how many times we fall flat on our face.

The practice of persistence is becoming rarer and rarer these days, because modern technology means there's usually a quick fix for everything. Can't be bothered cooking? Order Uber eats. Need something in a hurry? Same-day delivery. Feeling sad? Get a dopamine hit from social media.

Unfortunately, there's no quick fix for a spinal injury. I mentioned earlier that a spinal injury is a matter of centimetres. But it's also a matter of millimetres . . . that's how much a spine heals in a month's worth of rehab. One millimetre. I had nothing if I didn't have perseverance in those early rehabilitation sessions.

I FIGHT, YOU FIGHT

Sometimes I wouldn't see any improvement at all in my physical ability. I would show up at the gym day in and day out to do the same thing over and over again – and not get any better at it. But even if I wasn't seeing daily results, I knew the effort was compounding. I knew rewards were coming.

Remember that thing I said to Mum about wanting my arms back? Fast forward a year and I would be able to pick up a cup at Sushi Train for the first time. But it took a lot of steps to get there. I had started with the arm slings, moved on to the hand cycle, and before long I was getting my arm strength up by stacking cups during physio sessions (I stacked a whole lot of cups). My neural pathways were reforming and before I knew it, I was able to hold a ball against my chest. I could hold an apple against my chest, too, but I couldn't quite get it up to my mouth to take a bite. It was frustrating, to be so close and yet so far. But one day, while Tess and I were waiting for someone to pick us up to take us out for the day, she handed me an apple and told me to eat it.

'I can't,' I told her. 'You know I can't.'

'Just try,' she said. So I did. It took all kinds of strength and concentration to get that apple to my mouth, but after a dozen drops, it finally hit my teeth and I took a bite. It wasn't the best apple I've ever eaten, but it was definitely the sweetest. The taste of success.

To celebrate my win, Benji made me a spoon. Yes, a spoon. Once I was capable of eating on my own again, I could only do so with specially designed utensils that had finger holes to fit my hand exactly – and those spoons cost a couple of hundred dollars a pop. So Benji, being Benji, saw the challenge and spent about two hours making a replica. He was always making things growing up so this was nothing new, but he wanted to do his bit to help me. Benji's design was basically a regular spoon attached to a coat hanger bent in shape to make finger holes, and held together by tape and heaps of glue. Four years later, I'm still using a spoon my brother made me.

Once I could use my arms a bit more, I wanted to challenge myself. At the hospital, I'd been set up with a power chair – all I had to do was make the smallest hand gesture to get it to go anywhere I wanted to go. But I knew a power chair wasn't going to help me get stronger. The physio at Royal Rehab didn't think I was ready for a manual chair seeing as I couldn't even move the power chair at first, but I was pretty insistent. Okay, maybe I was stubborn. But eventually my physio caved and got me a manual chair. Win! The only problem was, I could barely move it. Getting to the gym, 20 metres away from my room, seemed like a mission to Mars. But I was up for it.

Every centimetre took a huge amount of time and effort. Although the hallway was flat, it didn't feel like that to me. In the manual chair, pushing as hard as I could, I felt every slight incline – every single bump was like a hurdle I had to clear. That first 20-metre trip to the gym must have taken me at least half an hour. But I kept at it, getting myself there and back, lap after lap after lap, always focusing on improving my speed.

And before long, I was already thinking about the next challenge. I was going to do a full lap of the rehab that would take me down the hallway, past the gym, past the nurses' desk, and back to where I'd started. Harrison was up for the challenge too, and soon we were calling our laps 'time trials' and logging our times, as if we were speed racers or elite athletes. In a way, we weren't too far off: we were just competing in a very specific sport.

At first, my laps took an eternity. I could have a twenty-minute conversation with the nurses as I slowly rolled my way past their desk at a snail's pace. 'Do you want some help?' they'd ask, watching me crawl along between their telephone calls. I shook my head. 'Are you *sure* you don't want any help? You're not really going anywhere . . .' the nurses would say, looking concerned when I was still in front of their desk ten minutes later. They definitely thought I was a total psycho, spending my days crawling down the hallway at the speed of paint drying. But help was the last thing I had in mind. 'I've got this,' I told them. Because I knew that every minute of effort was making me stronger.

Harrison, who was further along in his recovery than I was, sometimes got behind me on our laps and nudged me along with his chair. If our time trials had been an Olympic sport, I'm pretty sure this would have been cheating, but mostly it was just fun. At the end of the day, the whole point of the laps was this: it didn't really matter how slow I was going, as long as I didn't stop. As long as I kept fighting to the finish line. Every centimetre was its own little victory, but the real reward was knowing that I hadn't given up.

By the end of my stay in rehab, I could do a lap in three minutes and five seconds going clockwise, and three minutes and fifty seconds going anticlockwise – my left arm is stronger, and that gave me an advantage on the corners. Not bad, I reckon. And yes, I did record each time trial on my phone notes.

Tess and I came up with a thing called, 'champagne moments' in rehab, which was basically all the milestones we wanted to celebrate with champagne. Beating my own personal best for a lap was definitely a champagne moment.

Another one was having a night out. This time, it was going to be a literal champagne moment if I had my way. But having a night out on the town isn't so simple when you're in rehab for a spinal cord injury. You can't just call an Uber and head to a pub or club. In order to even leave the building, you had to have a 'gate pass', which is basically a medical assessment done by your doctors and physios that meant you were allowed to go out.

I FIGHT, YOU FIGHT

Of course, I'd only been in rehab a few days when I started angling for a gate pass. The doctors and nurses didn't think it was a good idea – I still had a neck brace on, after all, and I guess they had a point. But I wouldn't take no for an answer. So on 4 December 2018 – about two months after my injury – my mates busted me out of there (if only for the night). We headed out to eat ribs at Hurricane's and watch a movie. And let me tell you, when you've been stuck inside pretty much around the clock for weeks and weeks on end, you really appreciate being able to do something as simple as enjoying a meal with mates. Sure, I couldn't eat the ribs without help, but I was out! I was free! And suddenly I realised how much I had taken for granted before my accident. Just being out and about, watching people walk by, chatting to the waiter – all of it was magic to me in that moment. And the ribs were pretty good too!

A little later, I scored an overnight gate pass for Christmas and was able to spend my first night away from the centre with my family at home – with thanks to the Riverview boys and their parents for raising money to deck the halls with makeshift ramps and a special bed to make it accessible for me. It turns out Zac's best mate's grandpa was *the* Harvey of Harvey Norman, and he sorted us out with couches, a huge TV, and of course, it was all hooked up with voice activation for me. One of the Riverview mums was an interior designer, and the whole crew had transformed a downstairs room into an accessible space for hanging out. It was really special, walking in and seeing what everyone — friends and strangers — had done for me and my family.

The only thing we didn't have at the house was a hoist, which is basically a small crane that you use to lift someone from a wheelchair into a bed, or vice versa. So on Christmas eve, my dad was on duty to tuck me in. He lifted me out of my chair . . . and just about crash tackled me onto the bed. It was stacks on, after that. I reckon my dad could actually have been a decent flanker. Anyway, the important thing is that I made it to bed, because the next morning, Christmas Day, was full of so many familiar comforts: we woke up early to unwrap presents, and then some of our extended family showed up for the classic ham, prawns, oysters for lunch. Plus potato bake, a personal favourite. And my nanna's caramel slice remained the best thing I have ever tasted. But there were a few surprises, too. Even though I was still in a power chair and a neck brace, my nanna got the go ahead to let me have a beer — I was still sixteen, remember! — and soon enough, well, let's just say that I was feeling pretty merry. I even won a Christmas bon bon battle with her by holding it in my teeth, really tight. But the best part of that Christmas was still to come.

My friend Zane texted me late in the afternoon, to see what I was up to and ask if I wanted to come over. It was turning into a pretty snoozy Christmas afternoon, so I said

I FIGHT, YOU FIGHT

yes. He rigged up one of the dodgiest ramps I've ever seen out of two bits of wood to get me down to his back deck, but once I got there, I had the perfect view of him and a few other friends playing footy in the backyard. It was a really warm night, and I was wearing compression stockings to help with my circulation, seeing as I wasn't moving much, so I asked someone to take them off me. And that was when I felt it. A fly, landing on my big toe.

'Jayden! Guess what? I can feel it, I can feel that fly!' It was a Christmas miracle. Up until that point, I had only been able to feel extremes, like if there was intense pressure on my lower limbs. But if I could now finally feel something as soft and light as a fly landing on my foot . . . was there a chance that I would one day get some movement back, too?

And then, in early January 2019 – about three months after the accident and three months of showing up for physio twice a day – something totally unexpected happened. My big toe moved. On its own. It was the first sign of nerves passing the break in my neck. It was the most surreal thing, almost as if I could feel the nerves surging from my brain, through my body, straight to the big toe on my right foot. I focused on it as hard as I could and suddenly there it was – a flicker in my toe. A flicker of hope.

I decided that my next champagne moment was going to be moving my leg for the first time. If I could move my toe, surely I had it in me to move my leg, right? I kept focusing on my toe, and the bigger mission of my leg. And then, one night in February, I had been hanging out with Tess in her room, just watching TV and chewing the fat. She told me her story – how she'd ended up here. Tess had been swimming in a lake in Geneva when she'd suddenly lost feeling in her arms and legs. She had no idea what was happening, but she was sinking fast. And it was sheer willpower that came to her rescue. Somehow, she managed to claw her way out of the water. She could have drowned, but she had dug deep to survive.

Touched and inspired by the story Tess had just told me, I rolled out of her room and into mine, which was lit up by the Himalayan salt lamp she had given me. I was thinking about what she had said – about all the pure mental strength it took her to haul herself out of that lake, so she could keep living.

I pressed the buzzer to let the nurses know I was ready to go to bed, and as I was waiting for the nurse, sitting alone in the middle of my room on my wheelchair, I looked down at my right quad. Thinking about Tess's own strength, sitting there in silence and staring at my legs, I felt this intense power come over me that told me to try and move. 'Just try,' I could hear her saying, like she had on the day with the apple. And suddenly, a sense of clarity washed over me and I knew what I had to do. If Tess could get to the surface and save herself from drowning, then surely I could tense my quad? I focused directly on my right quad harder than I had ever focused on anything before, and after squeezing with every single bit of energy and power I had, I felt this weird, indescribable wave of something that rushed through me and . . . Yes! There it was! My right quad twitched! It was the tiniest twitch ever, but I didn't care . . . there was movement! Evidence of a neural pathway that I thought was gone forever. I yelled as loud as I could.

A nurse arrived, and I asked her to get Tess.

'I've got to show you guys something!' I told them both, and then I did it again. I wasn't dreaming, they saw it too! Tess started crying; I started crying. Eventually after a lot of tears and excitement, the nurses transferred me into the bed using a big ceiling hoist. I landed right in the middle of the bed on my back with my legs laid out in front of me like a butterfly stretch. As I lay there, I thought to myself, surely if I can tense my quad in my wheelchair, I can tense my quad in bed. So again, I squeezed. And this time, something even more spectacular occurred. This time it wasn't just a flicker in my quad, but I was able to straighten my whole leg! I didn't go to sleep, I couldn't go to sleep – instead we stayed up all night taking videos of me moving my quad.

We Facetimed Mum and Dad so they could share in the champagne moment. Of course, they cried too. With Tess's inspiration, and my own pure determination, I had made my leg move and defied my diagnosis. It was pure euphoria – way better than MDMA could ever be (not that I've tried it!).

After gaining this movement in my leg, I knew I had to capitalise on it. I didn't know if this flicker was going to be all I ever got back, but while I had that neural pathway established, I had to keep working on it. It was a blessing – I knew that – and I wanted to see how far I could take it. I dared myself to flirt with the idea of maybe one day standing up on my own, or even taking some steps. I knew how unlikely this was, but this experience had taught me something valuable: that my mind was more powerful than I had ever realised, much more powerful than my body had been even when I was smashing it on the sports field.

I got so addicted to that idea of getting back more movement that I couldn't stop thinking about all the possibilities this new neural pathway could open up for me. I became so obsessed with tensing my quad that I found myself doing it nearly every five seconds of the day, even to the point that it prevented me from sleeping properly. It just felt so good to be able to move it on my own; to be able to voluntarily contract my leg. It's probably hard for most people to imagine, finding joy in the movement of a muscle, but I never wanted to lose that feeling again – or forget what it felt like – so I couldn't stop myself tensing it. If five or more seconds passed since I had squeezed it, I'd think to myself, *We haven't done that in a while, better squeeze it again!* or *I should squeeze again just to make sure I don't lose it!* I was hooked. What else could I flex? *C'mon, Alex, there's work to do.*

I FIGHT, YOU FIGHT

We moved to leg exercises in the gym.

I was slowly regaining my independence and coming to terms with this new way of living, but in the midst of all that I still just wanted to be a kid. It was June 2019, and my mates were all going to an under-eighteens music festival. Despite all the obstacles and risks, I built up the courage to say yes, and I'm glad that I did. Because it's not every day that you get to go crowd surfing in a wheelchair with A$AP Ferg playing.

When we arrived at the festival, my mates and I hung back a bit on the fringes, steering clear of the crowds. But they were pretty keen to get me into the mosh pit. At first, I thought it was too risky, too hard – the crowd was really going off. But it turns out that nothing is too hard when you have the best mates on the planet. I finally gave in, and before I knew it, my mates had got into a V-formation around my chair, three on each side. We sliced through that crowd like a spear and made it all the way into the centre of the mosh pit.

It was a weird feeling, being in the centre of that thrashing crowd. In my chair, I was so much lower than everyone else, and I couldn't see much of what was happening on the stage. Everyone was towering above me, I felt small. But as we watched other people crowd surfing, my mates started telling me to get up there – all of them except Connor, who had lost himself somewhere in the crowd. (Connor has been my mate since preschool, and he's super high energy, optimistic – always gravitating towards a good time or the scene of the crime – so of course he went off into the mosh that night, getting stuck into it in the way only Connor can.)

'Go on, we'll lift you up!' my mates were saying.

'No way!' I said at first. It was way too risky. But as the music surged, I put my fear aside and took the risk. 'Whatever, let's do it!'

My friends swarmed around me and next minute, I was high above the crowd, looking out over thousands of people, with a perfect view of A$AP Ferg singing 'New Level'. I was on a new level, too. With the help of my friends, I'd gone from feeling low, small and inferior, to being on top of the world. I had been elevated to a new level, and I was absolutely loving it. I could see everything – including Connor, who was about 20 metres away from the rest of us. He must have heard the cheers because his head snapped around, and he copped an eyeful of me surfing the crowd, high above everyone's heads. I guess he was pretty impressed, because he started waving and screaming at me; he even took a photo to immortalise the moment.

And Connor wasn't the only one who was impressed with my crowd surfing antics – a little later in the night, I was back at it again and Future was playing. He paused in the middle of a song to point at me and say, 'This dude's crazy!' And maybe it was a crazy thing to do, crowd surfing in a wheelchair with my shirt off at my first ever festival on top of thousands of randoms, but I don't regret it for a second. The crowd roared.

I rolled back into rehab at 3 am with my mate Jayden in tow. He signed me back in and we pissed ourselves laughing when we realised there was no nurse available at that hour to transfer me into bed. So, drunk as he was, Jayden rose to the challenge. It only took about thirty minutes longer than usual, and, as he tucked me in, we just looked at each other laughing and yelling, 'Best. Night. Ever!' It was lying there after he left when I realised I still had all my best days ahead of me. That's what a champagne moment can do for you.

My crowd surfing experience also made me realise something else. Up until this point, I had seen how my recovery had inspired people through social media, but it had always seemed like a strange side effect – I wasn't going out of my way to change the world or teach anyone a lesson. I had just been letting things happen, and my cousin Carolyn had even been the one posting to my Instagram account for me. But when I started to think about how much my mates had supported me and fought for me – literally formed a guard to march me into the mosh pit, and then held me up in their arms – I realised that I had something to say. I fight, you fight. My friends could see how hard I was fighting to get better, and they fought for me, too. So, a few days after the festival, I posted the epic photo Connor had taken and wrote a long post:

Life has been a long, bumpy road of late. I am now ready to get into the driving seat of this page to show you that life hasn't limited me, I've only just begun. I feel like I have been living in a dream, and am only now just coming to terms with what lies ahead of me. What I've realised is that I don't have a disability, I have an ability. I want to show the world that you can't sit around and wait for something better to happen, better is now. If not now, when? If not me, who? You're the CEO of your life and I am taking over as my own CEO because I want to show the world that there are no limits to any of us, so let's wake up every morning together, dream big and realise that life is a gift and you have to make the most of it. I hope that I inspire the world to make it a better place. Let's get up and ROLL OVER LIFE TOGETHER.

I cannot thank you all enough for all your words, wishes, support and donations. Every night I read the comments which inspire me to dream big and wake up every day to take on the next challenge ahead and much, much more. Let's work together and accomplish the things that we have only dreamed of, and help everyone else along the way.

One thing I know to be true is that I am not what happened to me, I am what I choose to become. #ifightyoufight #bigthingstocome

I FIGHT, YOU FIGHT

What I really appreciate now is not just those incredible nights out with my friends, but just the simple fact that they're always there. The rate at which my mates showed up to rehab never slowed down; their visits only increased in frequency. And they soon realised that rehab was a pretty cool place for us to hang out.

You know how in every group of teenagers, there's usually one house where everyone always seems to congregate? For us, that was the duck pond at the rehab centre. Sometimes we had up to fifty people down by the duck pond, at all hours of the day and night, with tunes and a BBQ and lots of laughs. One of my footy mates, Dylan, even met his girlfriend down there. The days by the duckpond weren't as exciting as my death-defying crowd surfing experience, sure, but they're some of my favourite and most formative memories. I wish I could tell you more about what went on there, but the unspoken rule was: what happens at the duck pond stays at the duck pond.

~

Six months after that first flicker in my big toe, and after months of relentless training, day in and day out, I finally developed enough strength to do a leg extension . . . against gravity. It was June by this point, and the progress I had made with my legs made me brave enough to dare to dream of one day being able to stand up again. I refused to let go of that dream.

NeuroMoves gym is where I remember a lot of my 'firsts'. It's a specialist facility in Lidcombe for people living with neurological conditions and physical disabilities. One morning, I rolled into the gym, and they had me doing some pretty standard exercises at first. About half an hour in, though, one of the physios turned to me and said, 'Right, we're going to get you to try and stand now.' I was taken aback. Up until that point – through all my rehab and physio appointments and training sessions – I had never been told I was going to try standing. I thought he was joking. I laughed.

But the physios seemed confident . . . and they were the experts, right? Standing for the first time required strength outside of myself, both literally and figuratively. It took about five people to get me into position, plus a standing frame, a waist belt and eight stimulation pads. The stimulation pads were strapped around my limbs to help my muscles contract as I moved with the help of everyone else – like a TENS pad on steroids.

The physios manoeuvred me onto the edge of a remote-controlled bed and hooked me up to a hoist. The bed was positioned as high off the ground as it could be so I didn't have to squat too deeply to get me up. In total I had five physios helping me stand – one was sitting behind me to hold me in a sort-of seated position, as I had no core strength to do it myself. Another was in front of me; his knees bound to my knees with a piece of foam in between our shins in case my legs gave way. Two physios were positioned either side of me, mainly for balance, and a fifth physio was holding the standing frame in place.

By the time I was supposed to stand, I realised the bed was so high off the ground I was practically already there. I was just a few centimetres away from standing for the first time, and when my feet hit the ground I wish I could tell you I felt like a superhero. I actually felt like one of those inflatable tube men you see out the front of car dealerships whose arms flail around everywhere. Like I had no control. My chest stuck out too far, my bum was too far back, my legs were bent and shaky and I swayed from one side to the other, unable to find any balance.

The emotion of it all was a total paradox. Up there, I realised that I had forgotten what it felt like to take up that much vertical space. Everyone was surprised by how tall I was. I felt independent and grounded. And yet, I wasn't independent at all – I was only standing thanks to the horsepower of five other people. But it was a start.

I took my first steps at NeuroMoves in July 2019 – eight months after the accident. This time, they strapped me into a hoist positioned in front of a treadmill. Ties were fastened around my legs, my groin, my torso and my shoulders, which then lifted me out of my chair into a standing position, the hoist supporting my entire weight.

I wasn't as excited this time; my overwhelming feeling was frustration. This was six months after I stood for the first time, and I remember thinking how stupid it was that I needed six people surrounding me just to help me stand up and then take a few steps – *there's no way I'm ever going to be able to do this on my own*, I thought. *All of this, just to take a step, and I'm not even the one doing it . . . they're doing it.*

One physio took my right leg, one took my left leg, one supported my torso, one operated the treadmill and one – very importantly – held a mirror out in front of me so I could see how sick I looked walking for the first time in over a year. The physio operating the treadmill started it up at a snail's pace and the others began lifting, pushing and bending my dead-weight legs at my knee and ankle joints in a way that almost resembled walking.

It was slow and laborious to start, but after about a minute the six of us had found our rhythm – we were an in-sync walking machine! They were all playing their parts, but I was walking. *I was walking!* I looked up at the mirror in front of me and drank it in. I couldn't see the six physios corralled around me. Or I chose to ignore them. Because I was walking, and it felt so natural to walk; so normal. I was liberated, it felt like freedom. I felt like my old self. I can't believe I had ever taken this, *walking*, for granted.

CHAPTER 10
IN TESS'S WORDS

I cried at every one of Alex's champagne moments. From the first time he moved his leg, to when he first held and ate an apple on his own. And even when he did his first speech in front of a thousand people. Don't even ask me to go into the first time Alex stood up out of his chair to hug me. These moments will stay with me forever.

Despite how monumental our friendship was – and still is – I don't actually remember the first time I *met* Alex. It wasn't some earth-stopping, soul-recognising-soul moment. Rather, we were both in the same place, at the same time, for reasons we wish didn't bind us together.

The events that brought Alex into my life are painful to think about. Back in 2018, I had landed a new job and moved to Switzerland. But while on a skiing trip with my new colleagues, I was skiing down a black run when I crashed head-first into a wall of snow. I was able to get up and ski off the mountain, but I remember thinking: *This isn't good.* My body felt different. For months, I had strange symptoms ranging from pins and needles and headaches to a loss of feeling in my legs and wetting myself daily. I was so driven to make a good impression at my new job that I carried on – buying emergency underwear seemed like an easier option than confronting what was happening to me. Then, one day, I couldn't feel my hands.

I was in and out of the hospital for seven months. I had two major spinal cord surgeries and spent three months learning to use my body again. Every scan and test led me further into the abyss. I was only thirty-two years old, I wasn't married, I didn't have kids, and I had just flown halfway around the world for this new job. But instead of forging the exciting career I had envisioned, I found myself alone in bed and unable to move. My life had boiled down to this. I was at rock bottom.

I had heard about Alex through my family, who would sit at my bedside telling me stories of the hallways beyond my cordoned-off section of the hospital. They told me about the boy who had been in a rugby accident who *always* had scores of visitors there to see him, and whose Instagram had attracted 10,000 followers in just a few days. The handle was @ifightyoufight. Those words really struck me, but I had so much going on that I don't think I really processed them in that moment. It was only later that I understood their true meaning.

In moments of pain and darkness it can be so easy to lose ourselves, and I can honestly say that without Alex, I am not sure where I would be right now. About two weeks post-surgery, I managed a small 'walk'. I was in a lot of pain, but I was also drugged up and ready to take on the challenge of

My christening at Holy Spirit Catholic Church in North Ryde in 2003.
From left to right: Mum, Zac, Dad, me in Nan's arms, Pop.

Riding my favourite red bike around our house in East Ryde.

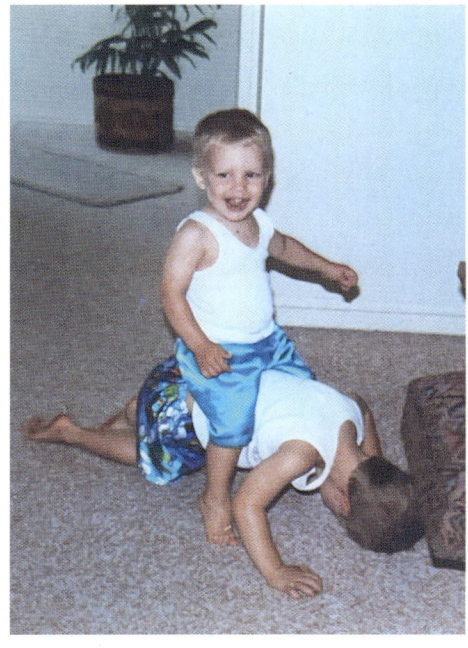

Dominating Zac in a fight at Nan and Pop's house in Townsville, Queensland.

Ice cream was always the fastest way to get Zac (left), Benji (right) and me to stop fighting.

Mitchell Moses (left) and Curtis Sironen (right) presenting me with the award for Man of the Match and Player of the Series.

Me and Zac on my first day of high school at St Ignatius' College Riverview in 2015.

Surfing at Waikiki Beach, age 11, on a family trip to Hawaii.

On a paddleboard at Avoca Beach, New South Wales, age 14.

Rocking the budgies on a day out on the boat in Manly. From left to right: Me, my friend Charlie, Zac, Benji.

Christmas Day on the boat with family in 2016. From left to right: Dad, Pa, Uncle Brian, me, Nanna, Benji.

Noble family dinner at a groovy Japanese restaurant in Manly in 2016.

Attending house mass with my family at St Ignatius' College Riverview, at the beginning of Year 10.

With Mum and Dad, celebrating a win in the Under 16 State Championships after beating the ACT Brumbies and scoring a 50-metre try in the grand final.

Playing in the Under 16 New South Wales schoolboys rugby team at a tournament in Narrabeen, with Dally (left), and Hamish (centre).

Doing a kick and chase to score the game-winning try in the Under 16 rugby league grand final for the Holy Cross Rhinos at Redfern Oval, against the South Eastern Seagulls.

Setting up a try in the Under 16 GPS schoolboy rugby team.

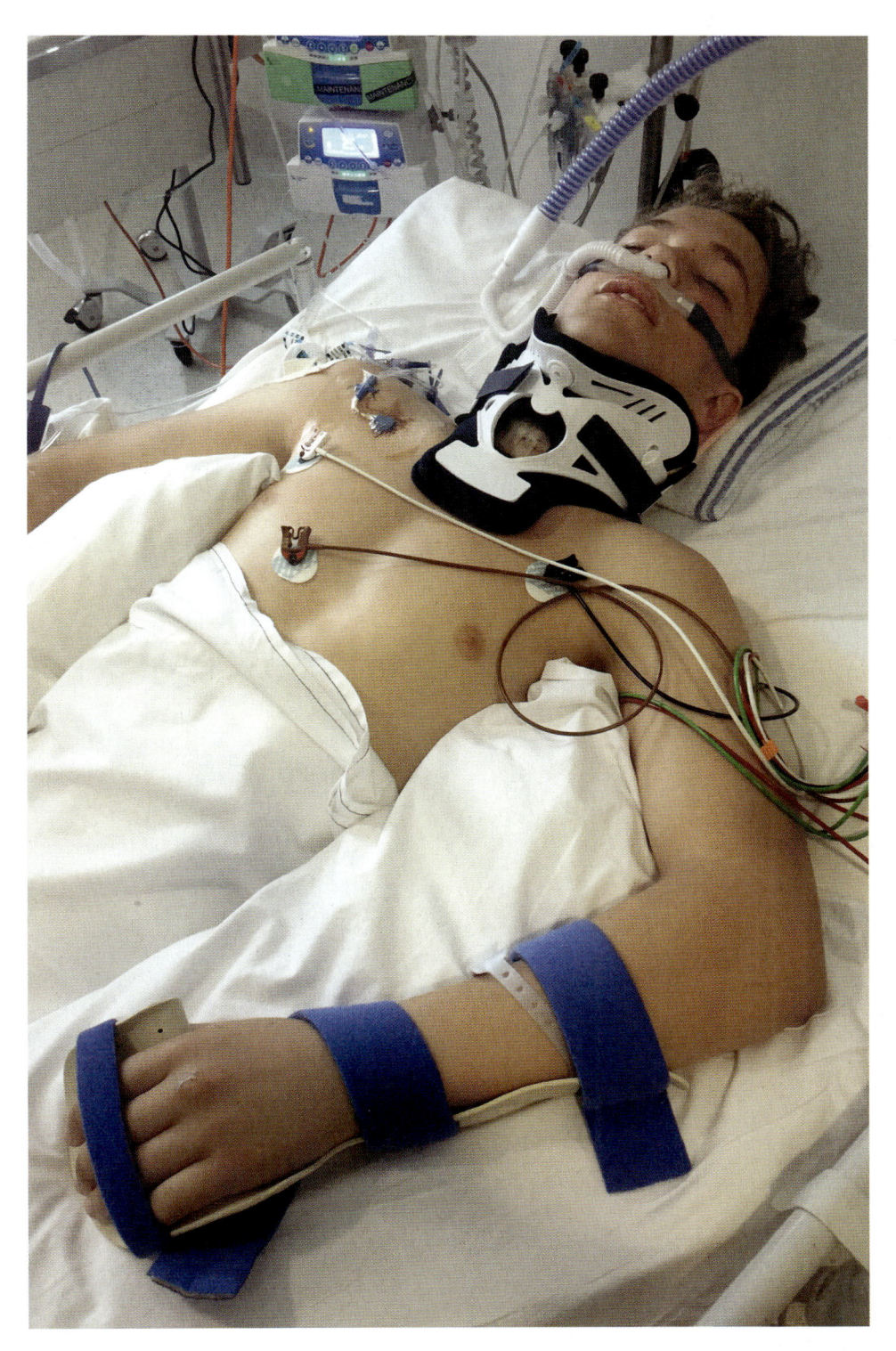

In a four-day coma in the intensive care unit at Royal North Shore Hospital after an eight-hour spinal surgery.

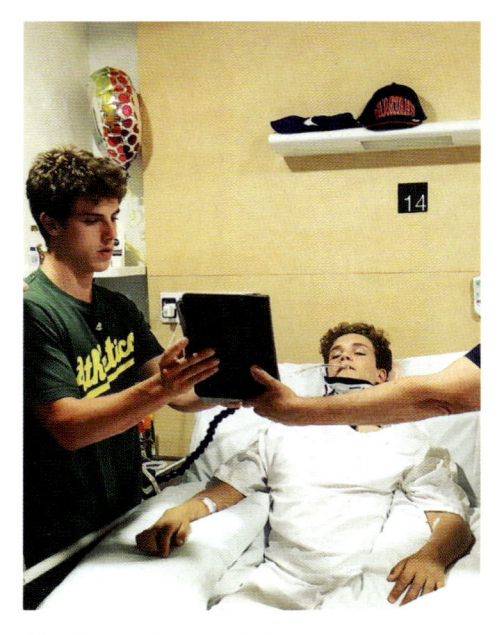

Six days after my injury, Zac is showing me all the messages of support I received – I'm unable to move anything except my eyes.

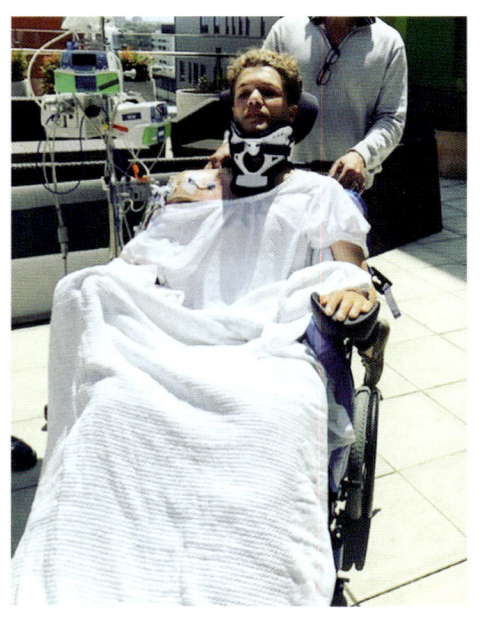

My first time out of bed, nine days after the accident. It was a process all right, but it was exciting to see some sunlight.

On the balcony of the spinal unit, twelve days after my injury, when my friends were finally allowed to visit. From left to right: Eddie, Jett, Bella, James, Ryan, Henry, Cassi and Connor (standing), Nic, Tom and me.

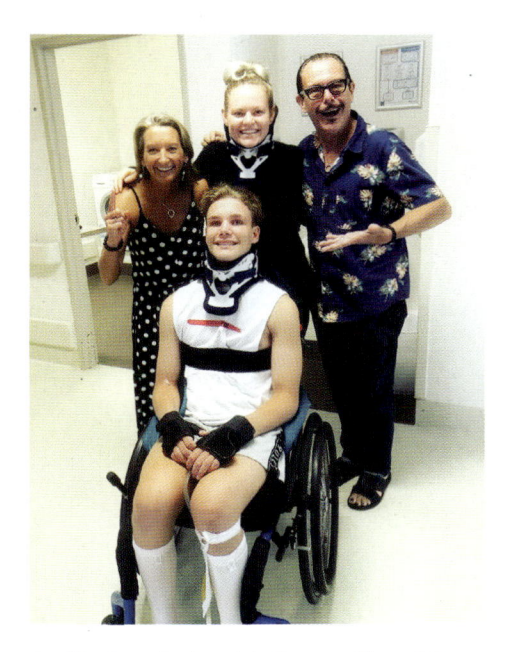

At Ryde rehab with Layne Beachley (left), Tess (centre back) and Kirk Pengilly (right), about a week after I got my first manual wheelchair.

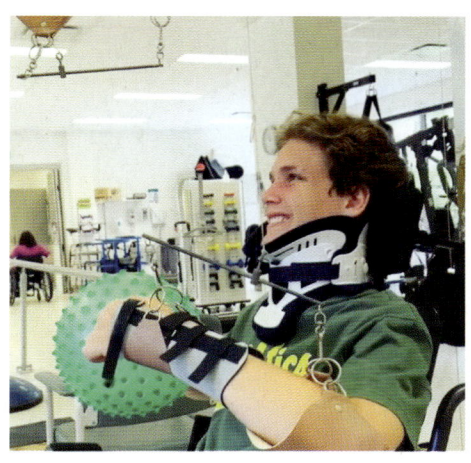

An occupational therapy session at Ryde rehab, trying to hold a ball in the air – with a lot of assistance from the slings helping me lift my arms.

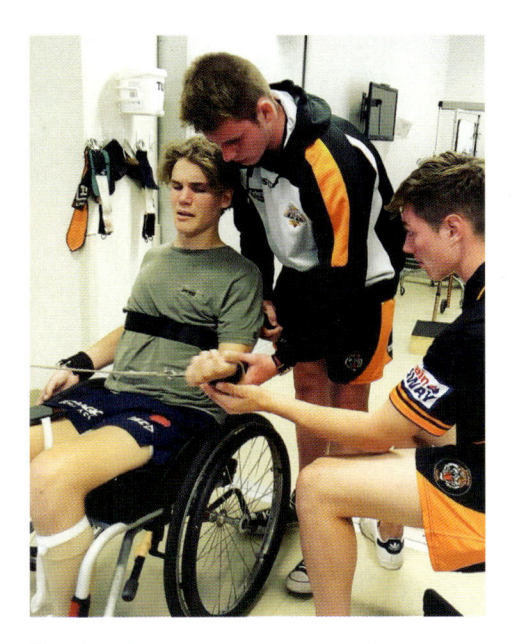

Putting in an extra gym session at night with Henry (centre) and Zayne (right), who visited after their own footy training.

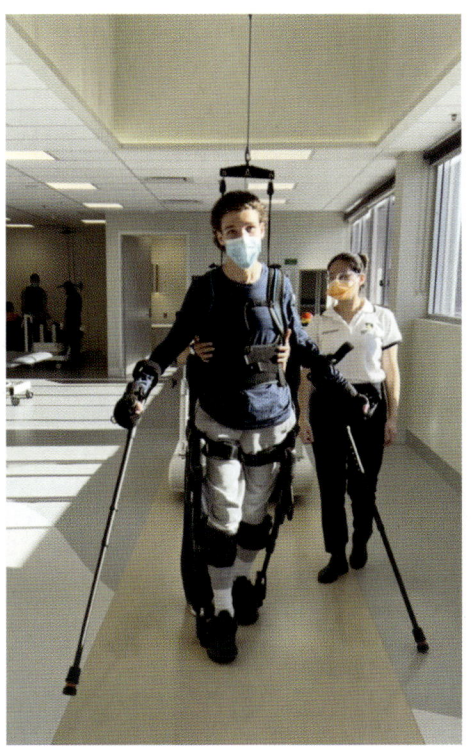

Using the incredible exoskeleton in Ryde rehab's flagship advanced technology hub to take some steps!

My first time back in the water at the beach with my mates – one year and four days after my accident. From left to right: Connor, Sam, Dylan, me, Nic, Zayne, Jake.

About to hit the surf again, just over a year after my accident. Benji and Zac standing up the back, and my two surf instructors by my side.

At my mate's holiday house on the Central Coast, about to go jet-skiing!

Heading back to Manly Sailing Club with my sailing instructor, after making it across the heads of Sydney Harbour about one year after my accident.

My first time skydiving, about two years after my injury – I was freaking out . . .

. . . but we all landed safely after sharing one of the best experiences of our lives. From left to right: Dylan, Jayden, Tom, Tess on my lap, Zac, Dad, Mack, Connor.

The Alex Noble Gala event on 23 February 2021, when over 800 people came together to show their support – one of the most special nights of my life.

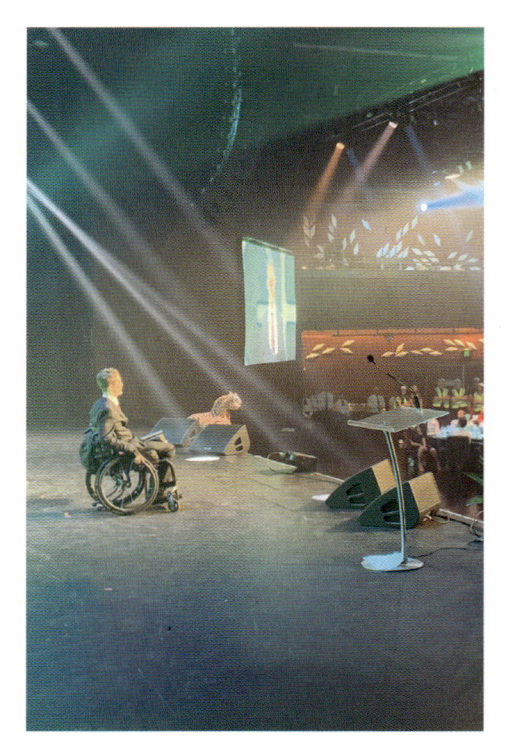

Up on stage to thank everyone at the Alex Noble Gala event.

Celebrating behind the scenes with Mum, Benji, Tess, Zac and Dad.

Dressed to impress for the Everest Carnival event at Randwick Racecourse, raising money for Spinal Cure Australia.

Party at Sydney's Ivy Penthouse with Connor (left), Dylan (centre back) and Jayme (right).

With Brooke at Aster Bar, our favourite rooftop bar, with one of the most spectacular views in Sydney.

Crowd-surfing in front of Future, A$AP Ferg and thousands of other people at my first ever festival.

Overheating in 40° weather at the Pantheon in Rome with Dylan, moments before I had my favourite meal: penne arrabiatta with extra chili, bacon and olives.

Roaming Amsterdam's red-light district in 2022. From left to right: Zac, Alex L, me, Dylan, Connor, Aaron.

Riding on a camel with Dylan in the desert near Dubai.

Straight from a private boat to a VIP table at O Beach club in Ibiza (with a 6-litre bottle of vodka!) for my 20th birthday.

On a private boat cruising along the Amalfi Coast, Italy, in 2023. From left to right: Jayden, Santiago, me, Dylan, Gabby.

Eating pizza in front of the Eiffel Tower in Paris, with Dylan, Gabby and Jayden.

Celebrating my 21st birthday on Ios Island, Greece, eating the famous Greek gyros after a swim!

I FIGHT, YOU FIGHT

shuffling 20 metres to the ward's kitchen. When I finally got there, I was met by about fifteen kids all crammed into the tiny soulless space. And then I saw Alex. There he was with his sunnies on, surrounded by friends, music blaring. They all seemed so happy. I managed an awkward 'hello' before slinking off back to my room, wanting to disappear. I didn't know it yet, but those boys would soon be like family to me, and Alex like a little brother.

One by one, the patients at the hospital unit were slowly transferred to a rehab facility. I was struggling with my own physical and mental challenges, but I didn't see why I needed to be in rehab. The doctors had their own plan, though, and it involved hours of physiotherapy, occupational therapy, hydrotherapy – you name it, they had it. Alex, Harrison and I had rooms at the end of the same hallway, and we quickly formed a tribe. I like to think that the doctors put me there to look after the boys.

While the spinal cord unit at the hospital had felt like a transient place where we spent time drugged out of our minds and having constant tests and scans, there was a sort of unspoken understanding among everyone who made it to rehab that we were in it for the long haul, so we might as well get to know each other. Our families all became friends, our therapists became lifelines, and the ward was taken over by the Alex Noble entourage. News crews, professional sports players, reality TV stars, celebrities, businesspeople – all there to support Alex and capture the magic that was building around him. I watched in awe.

The constant stream of visitors pouring in and out of Alex's room might have pissed some neighbours off, but it was the opposite for me. All of these people from the outside world rotating in and out became my daily entertainment. It was a people-watcher's dream, and it was never lost on me how abnormal and special it was. At one point during our stay, one of the nurses even made a complaint to security that all of Alex's guests were disturbing the other patients. But, as the only patient in the same wing as Alex at the time, I made a point to tell security that the noise wasn't an issue at all. The droves of visitors continued, and I considered it a win. It was only the first example of the lengths I found myself willing to go to, to protect and care for this teenage boy. He had a life to live, and being paralysed was just a road bump. He was fighting, and we all needed to fight too.

If there is a place to find purpose, then rehab is it. While I could still walk and had limited use of my hands, I could see that everyone around me was facing more serious physical challenges. And I was painfully aware of how privileged I was to survive a spinal cord injury and still be able to use my arms and legs. I developed a kind of survivor's guilt. Knowing that the boys didn't have that luxury, I started acting as their arms and legs whenever I could. I helped when there wasn't a nurse available. I helped when it was something embarrassing or silly. I helped because helping gave me a reason to get up every day.

I knew that it frustrated Alex that he had to call and wait for a nurse every time he wanted to brush his teeth, so I started popping across to his room to help him do it instead. I also knew he didn't like the smell of the bacon the kitchen staff kept accidentally giving him for breakfast, so I'd get rid of it for him before it stunk his room out. I'd order UberEats, change the music when the wrong song came on, and remove the clocks from our rooms when the constant tick, tick, tick would get too much to listen to all day, every day. In the end, I think being able to perform these small tasks ended up helping me far more than it actually did them. If I could help, I still had a purpose. Even though I felt like I had lost everything, in time I came to realise that I had gained so much more.

As Alex, Harrison and I grew closer, we started to find more creative ways to keep ourselves entertained. I had brought a whole bunch of face masks with me to rehab, and one night I came up with the idea of hosting a 'spa night' in my room where I gave the boys facials. As part of my rehabilitation program, my doctors were keen for me to do as many practical things with my hands as possible, so I started hosting cooking classes for all the patients as well.

My room slowly became Alex's unofficial waiting room. He had a stream of visitors, therapists, and people lining up to see him, so, naturally, there was an overflow. As much as I really did want to disappear into my own despair, I welcomed everyone in – to debrief, to laugh, and to cry. And in welcoming everyone into my room, I also welcomed Kylie and Glen Noble into my life.

If you want to know where Alex's strength comes from, you only have to look at his parents. They were on a mission. Kylie was there to get her son back to his old life, get him back to school, and make sure he had all the support he needed. I watched her face things no mother should ever have to face. I can't even begin to explain every roadblock Kylie navigated – from changing school policies and procedures so that Alex could get back to class, to finding the computer software that would help him complete his studies, even selling the family home and installing lifts in their new place – all while running a business and looking after her two other boys.

While Kylie handled the day-to-day practicalities, Glen took charge of media coverage, raising funds for spinal cord injury research, and setting up Alex's foundation – all with the aim of helping his son. Naturally, when someone is injured or ill, you look for treatments, trials, and most of all: hope. Surely if we can put a man on the moon, we can find a way to fix a spinal cord? Sadly, this still isn't the case. But learning everything he could about Alex's condition was Glen's mission. I remember one day, Glen came into my room as he was having a conference call with the Christopher Reeve Foundation. He had just read about a new technology that was really promising – it sent stimulation into the spine, helping signals get through. And he was so excited to tell me about it, because, funnily enough, its name was TESS, Targeted Epidural Spinal Stimulation. I couldn't help but laugh. What if I was the cure to my own condition?

I think Kylie and Glen appreciated the fact that there was an adult staying next door to Alex – someone who could step in when they couldn't. I became someone they could lean on for regular updates, someone to vent to and share their pain, joy, frustration and confusion with. If I was a big sister to Alex, then I was an unofficial daughter to them. I also became close with Alex's brothers, and one night Zac and I took Alex out for steak to celebrate the small win of the day. We decided to make a list of all the things Alex wanted to achieve. You might think that this list would start with 'walking again', but that was too small for Alex. Skydiving, wakeboarding, bungee jumping – those were all on the list. I added writing a book, but humble Alex told me no one would be interested!

Alex has a way of making the hard moments funny, with a joke, a smile, a cheeky comment to disarm you or diffuse a difficult situation. His wisdom shone through, and he listened, *really listened*, to what people had to say, and then he acted on it. He took everything to heart. One night, I told Alex about something terrifying that had happened to me before my injury was diagnosed. I had lost feeling in my legs while swimming in Lake Geneva, and I was sure at one point that if I didn't find a way to move, I was going to drown. But somehow I managed to grab onto the ladder on the wharf and I just clung to it – unable to pull myself up – for what seemed a lifetime. I gathered myself and focused every single thought, every ounce of willpower and energy, on moving my legs. I needed one push to get me back onto the wharf. And I did it.

In true Alex fashion, he took this story and applied it. A few hours after he'd gone to bed for the night, he yelled at me to come into his room. He had moved his leg. Not a small flex of the muscle, a total push. I've never felt hope like that before. It's amazing how the movement of a leg can mean so much to someone, and yet it's something most of us take for granted every day. The world of spinal cord injuries is slow. Painfully slow. But Alex dedicated himself to this slow process every day, and we were with him all the way.

Most nights, Alex went out with mates, living as any sixteen-year-old should. But unlike most sixteen-year-olds, he still had to come back to rehab and wait to be put to bed by the nurses. While he was waiting, he'd visit me and we would have deep chats about life. It struck me how wise beyond his years he was. Alex reframed adversity with charm, wit, and a willingness to challenge anything that wasn't up to his standard. Sometimes it was hard to keep up with him and

I FIGHT, YOU FIGHT

his incredible drive to do better, to be better. But he does everything with such grace it's no wonder everyone is left in his wake, trying to catch up.

As the weeks and months rolled by, I watched the way Alex was with his friends. Alex was caring and kind to everyone around him despite what had happened to him, and it had a ripple effect. Alex's superpower is helping people become the best version of themselves. He was put here to help others. Suddenly, I could see it: a book, a movie, a speaking circuit, partnerships with Red Bull and Nike – Alex showing the world what is possible even when everything seems impossible. So, I went to work. I found dozens of people who had inspired others with their stories, and told him, 'This could be you!' Alex looked at me and said, 'Why would anyone want to hear my story?' But here we are.

Alex recently told me he found it annoying that he couldn't express how grateful he was for everything I have done for him. But I think it's the other way round: how can I thank him for the purpose he gave me when I needed it most, for trusting me with a part of his future, for believing in me? Alex motivates me to redefine strength and unearth purpose in the most unexpected places. His unwavering determination, coupled with the support of friends and family, has shown me the true meaning behind the words 'I fight, you fight'. Alex and I became each other's pillar of support, and through our intertwined battles we discovered the beauty of shared victories and the resilience that emerges when you let go in order to hold on, trusting those around you to pave a path forward.

For those on the arduous road to recovery that Alex and I have been travelling down, my advice is to embrace the power of connection. In the darkest moments, it's the bonds forged with others that light the way. Reach out, lean on one another – and never, ever underestimate the power of a helping hand.

In the time I've known Alex, we've celebrated numerous champagne moments together, from speaking in front of thousands of people, to filming documentaries and giving radio interviews. Alex was present when I met my future husband, he was beside us on our wedding day, and he shared in the joy when I welcomed my baby boy, Benji, into the world. Alex and his family have witnessed me at both my best and worst, always creating a space for me to just be.

I've learned that true heroism lies not in the absence of struggle, but in the courage to confront it head-on. Alex's journey has left an indelible mark on my soul, a testament to the enduring power of friendship, resilience, and the human spirit's capacity to triumph over adversity. And for all these reasons and many more, I couldn't be prouder to call myself an honorary Noble.

CHAPTER 11

GOING HOME

'Life is not easy . . . life's not fair – it never was, it isn't now and it won't ever be . . . get over it and get on with it.'
– Matthew McConaughey

After 270 days, I finally made it home the day before my seventeenth birthday, which was on 19 July, 2019. For my birthday, my best mates came over for a low-key dinner at home, and we were joined by a few new close friends I'd made at rehab. Nanna and Pa were there too, and Mum and Dad put on a big Lebanese spread. Dad also made a speech and we embraced the place that I could finally call home again.

But the transition to moving home from rehab wasn't easy by any stretch. For lack of a better word, I had become 'institutionalised'. Rehab had become home for me, so moving 'home' meant I was leaving round-the-clock care, other people who understood what I was going through, and what had become a safe space and a comfort zone for me in the nine months I was there. I also had everything I could ever want at rehab – a purpose-built gym, an ensuite that accommodated all my bathroom needs, benchtops and handles and light switches that I could reach; every meal prepared for me, and every day planned out.

Mum and Dad and my friends were constantly agitating to get me back home, but I didn't share the same sentiment. I was completely hesitant and unsure. At rehab, I wasn't different. I was in the majority. I wasn't isolated or misunderstood or stared at. I was around people that got it. And I couldn't be confident that would be the case when I got home and back to school, when I rejoined a world I hadn't been a part of for such a long time.

The first few weeks were scary and frustrating – I was back in my old life, but in a new body, as a new human in a world that wasn't made for me. I couldn't just grab a snack in the kitchen like I used to be able to, or turn on the TV, or close a door, or turn on a light. I couldn't enter a room on my own. My 'morning' and 'night' routine now took over two hours each with the help of a carer – an hour of that alone spent on using the toilet. Then there are things no one tells you about living with quadriplegia – like you totally lose homeostasis, which is how the body is able to cool itself down when it's hot, or warm itself up when it's cold, by doing things like sweating or shivering.

Any slight change in the weather I feel to my core and regularly sleep with a heater or fan on depending on the outside temperature. The problem is that if the temperature changes in the middle of the night, then I'm unable to turn the heater or fan off on my own. There have been times where I've lain awake for hours at a time in the middle of the night, debating with myself whether to call Mum, wake her up, and get her out of bed to help me. After tossing up what's worse – suffering through the heat, or the guilt of waking Mum up in the middle of the night – I usually choose to just lie there and tough it out.

I FIGHT, YOU FIGHT

I remember about two weeks after my accident having one of the first conversations with my doctors about *'The things I must remember now that I'm a quad'*, and foremost among those awful things was pressure sores. Pressure sores are basically when skin on a particular part of your body is damaged due to constant pressure or friction – a real problem for quadriplegics, who are sitting all day and unable to move their body out of uncomfortable positions on their own. Anyway, this doctor had a folder full of A4 images showing the progression of a pressure sore, starting as a pretty insignificant red mark at 'stage one' – something even able-bodied people would get on their bum from sitting down too long – to 'stage four', which was the tearing of the skin, 'stage five' when infection sets in, and 'stage six' . . . well, you don't even want to know about 'stage six'. The images were disgusting, and pressure sores quickly became my biggest fear.

I was told I could prevent pressure sores by 'pressure relieving', which is making sure not to put my weight on the same part of my bum for too long by doing things like leaning forward or to the side. During my morning and night routine when I get in or out of bed, my carer checks my back over for red marks. I am so scared of getting a pressure sore one day that I get the carer to check two or three times over and I always ask, 'Are you sure?', even when they've given me the all clear for the third time. I know my paranoia gets annoying, but paranoia is a lot better than a pressure sore.

One morning during rehab I did wake up with a red mark. I knew as soon as the nurse took a fraction too long to tell me there was nothing there. I could feel their eyes burning into my backside, noticing the red dot, then hesitating to confirm the news. The diagnosis meant I had to stay in bed, lying on my side, to refrain from putting any more pressure on the sore. And it was hard to predict how long it would take to clear, because the blood circulation in my body is not as good as it once was. I ended up needing to lie in that position from Thursday morning to Monday night. Five days straight. A nurse would come into my room every two hours of the day and night to check the sore and make sure nothing was touching it. For the entire time, my neck and shoulders were aching painfully. When I was finally allowed to sit back up, I promised myself I would never go through that again. Much later, I learned about another quad who had to lie on his side for seven years because of an infected pressure sore. Seven years!

You can see why I'm paranoid!

Pressure sores aside, I face a lot of challenges in my life. And the worst challenges are the ones people can't even see. Benji once said to me that I'm not facing these challenges because I deserve it; I'm facing them because I can take it. And I think he is right. I think I can handle it. I think I can take it. However, there is one thing that I can't take. There is one thing that destroys me. There is one thing that absolutely kills me. And that is when I – my disability and my challenges – affect the quality of other people's lives. When I'm a burden on others, a liability. Like when my friends can't run down to the sand and into the water because they choose to sit with me up on the pavement. Or when my family can't go somewhere because it is inaccessible for me. Or when I wake up Mum and Dad from their sleep because I need their help in the middle of the night. Or when my brothers have to stop what they're doing because I need help going to the toilet.

So often people try to make me feel better about my disability by making jokes like, 'You're so lucky, you don't have to do the washing up!' or 'It must be nice not having to cook!', but the truth is, not being able to help is one of the worst things about my injury. I hate more than nearly anything watching Mum, Dad, Benji and Zac clean up after dinner while I just sit around and watch. The only thing worse than not being able to help is needing to ask for help all the time. When I have to watch my family and friends do things for me to make my life more comfortable while I just sit there like a liability, unable to do them for myself. When I have to ask family or friends to help cut up my food. When I have to ask family or friends to help put my jumper on because I am freezing. When I have to ask my family or friends to rearrange my feet into a better position, or scratch my shoulder, or push down my knee. A lot of the time, I don't ask because I'm sick of always asking so much of them. I'd rather sit there, uncomfortable, in silence.

Speaking of comfort, I'm never completely comfortable. Even in the most seemingly comfortable and relaxing of circumstances – like lying in bed or relaxing watching the footy – my body is pretty much in constant pain. My thighs feel like dead weights against the seat of my wheelchair, my stomach always feels bloated because I have no core strength, and my feet are always swollen and sore. When I am in bed or on the couch – where most people are at their comfiest – I'm unable to adjust my position to relieve any pressure from my heels, legs, back and bum. Nerve pain shoots through my limbs all day long, and it feels like accidentally touching a hot plate and not letting go. The nerve pain is always there, but sometimes it can be really excruciating. It's worse when I'm wearing pants or shoes, so even on the coldest winter day, I'll wear shorts instead. My friends laugh at me for my preference for shorts, but they don't understand the reason for it. Because my pain isn't something I talk about; I hate to complain. It's not the approach to life I'd choose. I don't tell them my legs feel like they're on fire, I'd rather laugh along with them instead.

I used to take a medication known as Lyrica to help alleviate some of this pain. But the side effects caused me to feel fatigued and groggy. For a few years I weighed up what was worse – the chronic nerve pain or the debilitating fatigue – but I knew that in order to get where I was planning to go,

I had to be functioning optimally. So, I decided to get off the medication and just cop the pain. Before I was diagnosed a quadriplegic, I didn't even know what quadriplegia was, let alone what it felt like. I knew it meant you had to use a wheelchair, and that was about it. What I've learned is that living life as a quadriplegic extends far beyond just the inability to walk, and the hardest thing I had to grapple with was my difference. I was different. Different from who I used to be, and now different from everybody else. I used to think of myself as an alpha male, a sportsman, but now I felt like I was inferior, an outlier. And no one ever prepares you for how much you're going to get stared at in a wheelchair. Luckily, I didn't have to go out much once I got home – besides regular visits to the physio. I spent my days getting acquainted with the new house, and trying to find a new routine outside of rehab.

The home I returned to wasn't even the one I had left, although it wasn't too far away. The house I grew up in, where we lived before the accident, was in Tennyson Point – right near the rehab. It was convenient in some ways, though not in others. The main problem was that it was a five-storey house, and wheels don't go so well on stairs. Mum and Dad thought about putting in a lift, but the house was on a battle-axe block with a long, steep driveway, and it would have been impossible to navigate with a wheelchair.

As a family, I think deep down we all knew we were going to need a new home, but the reality was, house-hunting can be overwhelming at the best of times and we had already been through so much. Luckily, Mum's friend Jillian was well aware of my new accessibility issues and began the hunt on our behalf – somehow she found a place literally down the road from my childhood home that she thought would be perfect. Mum was reluctant at first, but Jillian forced her to check it out, and she was right, it was a winner. It was so close to where we used to live that I could still see our old house from my new bedroom window. We installed a lift and two portable ramps for accessibility, but even with the most accessible house in the world, I was still going to need a lot of help (but we did pop a bottle of Veuve Clicquot when the lift finally went in). But just as I was returning to my life, my family had to eventually return to their lives and couldn't be around all the time. And that meant I needed carers.

Let me tell you something about carers. They all suck at the start. And that's not their fault at all, it's more to do with the fact that every person in the world is different, and we all do things differently. Do you know the exact position someone's leg should be in for them to feel comfortable, or how they want their hair done? Do you know the precise amount of scrubbing someone needs in order to feel clean? Probably not. And neither does a new carer.

So, if you're someone who needs care, it's kind of your job to train your carer. And that's harder than you'd think – you're used to doing everything for yourself, just the way you like it, but conveying what you want to someone else is another thing altogether.

And sometimes, it can be frustrating. Say your leg is itchy. You know exactly where to scratch it, but you can't. You can narrow it down for someone – *just below the knee, a little lower, over to the left, no, the other left!* – but for whatever reason, they just can't quite hit the spot. Now imagine this scenario applied to just about everything in your life: moving your legs to a comfortable position, adjusting your pants so that you're sitting properly, washing your body, and so on. Sure, you can keep your carer giving instructions, but you don't want to sound fussy or unappreciative – after all, they're trying to help you. So sometimes, it's better to just cop it how it is and say thanks.

As a carer, it's their job to care for you, but it's your job to teach them how to do it. It's a partnership. And the best carers have a very special skill: they never make it feel like a job at all. The best carers are just like good mates, although sometimes it can take a hot minute to get the friendship going.

Back when I was still in rehab, I was pretty resistant to the idea of having a carer at all. In fact, I almost blew off one of the best carers I've ever had. Let's just say it was a bit of a miscommunication. I was down at the tennis courts with a bunch of mates, and this guy rocked up. All of a sudden, he was standing next to us and joining in the conversation like he was part of the group. And we were like, 'Dude, who the hell are you?' Thankfully, we didn't actually say as much. Still, this guy kept on chatting up a storm, and he didn't take the hint that we thought he was a bit of a blow-in.

After a long and awkward while, the guy finally introduced himself as James, and told me that he was potentially going to be my carer.

'What's that?' I asked, not sure I had heard him right.

'Your mum set up this meeting for us, to see if we were a good fit. If it works out, I'm going to help you out in the mornings.' Mum had obviously forgotten to tell me about this meeting with James. The poor guy was there just trying to keep the appointment and we were all blowing him off!

'I don't need someone to help me in the mornings,' I told James. I was oblivious to my own needs, I had literally no clue what it would be like outside of rehab. 'I've got my mates.'

He looked amused. 'Your mates are great, but they're not going to be with you every second of the day. I could be there when they're not.'

It was a bad beginning, but James ended up being an amazing carer. He came four days a week for a whole year. He was a really good bloke, especially for turning up on day one after we were so rude to him at the tennis courts. And he was right, too. I *did* need someone to help me out in the mornings. Without carers, I'd probably still be in bed.

Since James, I've had lots of different carers. My support coordinator, Lee, was once my carer herself. These days, she's in charge of managing my NDIS plan, finding the medical products I need and ultimately, she's the person I fall back on if I need anything at all. She's super chill and has helped me so much over the years. And after interviewing and training carer after carer, I now have a great group helping me out.

One of my carers, Brooke, really took the role to a whole new level. She's not just a carer, she's one of my closest friends. She also happens to be my chauffeur, my chef, and sort of my everything. Brooke is one of the most easy-going people in the world, and we can talk about absolutely anything. Brooke knows all my quirks and secrets. She knows that when I have a house of my own some day, my requirements include an indoor and outdoor fire pit, plus a huge garden with fruit trees and a veggie patch. And it's got to have a gentlemen's room as my office, where I can sip whiskey and smoke cigars while listening to jazz on my record player after making multi-million dollar business deals. Brooke also knows that I have to have an acai bowl at least once a week. She knows that every night before bed, I like to listen to a song by . . . Okay, *that* secret is staying a secret. But you get the idea.

Brooke and I hang out all the time, even when she's not on shift. In so many ways, she liberated me – without her in my life, I couldn't do a lot of the things I'm doing. Because the thing you need to know about Brooke is that she's okay with spontaneity. Usually, when you have support workers, it's all about planning. You have to tell them when you want to go out and where, what time you're going to bed – you have to plan out your time, and it has to fit into their schedule as well. But that's not how life goes for most people. Do you always know the exact time you're going to want to go to bed, or when you're going to feel like going for a drive, or a drink with a friend at the pub, or when you're going to want to watch the sunset? I bet you don't, and I don't either.

With other carers, I just can't do those things when I want to do them. Everything has to be planned down to the minute. But with Brooke, I got a real friendship, and I also got my freedom back. I can just ring up Brooke, and she'll be there for me, ready to go for a cup of tea, or have a picnic by the water, watch the sunrise or the sunset, go to the beach, go out for lunch or just drive around the block. She's always up for an adventure. You may not even realise what a luxury it is to be spontaneous, but it's something I really value, and I couldn't be more grateful that Brooke has brought it back into my life. Without her, I can honestly say I would not be doing half the things I'm doing today.

On a more practical note, she's also a great person to call when I'm hungry. When we first met, Brooke was definitely not the most confident cook in the kitchen. In fact, she'll tell you that she *hates* cooking. But I made it my mission to help her, and together we've conquered caponata, Chicken McNuggets (or at least, a healthier version of them), dumplings and even sushi. The way we roll (yes, that's a sushi pun) is that I do all the organisation and she does the actual cooking. I read out the recipes and give suggestions while she gets her hands dirty prepping the food. Some would call us the brains and the brawn, but I just say we make a pretty awesome team.

It would be amiss of me not to also mention Stacey. Stacey has been in my life since kindergarten, a good friend of Mum's because she had a son the same age as Benji. But Stacey didn't take a leading role in my life until my accident. My early memories of Stacey involved her sitting around the kitchen with Mum having a cheese plate and glass of wine while the younger boys played together. These days, Stacey often jokes that I didn't say more than two words to her in between getting home from school and training, saying a quick hello to Mum, getting changed, and then heading out again with my mates.

It was Mum's idea to approach Stacey when they were looking for carers on my return home from rehab. What I didn't realise at the time was Stacey was fighting her own demons when Mum approached her, and taking on a role as one of my carers gave her something else to focus on during what was a tough time for her. Stacey had lost her husband unexpectedly only four years earlier, and was raising two boys a little younger than me. I know their family was struggling to find their feet again after their loss, but Stacey always says that spending time with me and listening to my perspective on life has inspired and helped her when times were tough. Sometimes I like to think that Stacey needed me as much as I needed her.

Stacey has done my bedtime routine for going on four years now. Every night, she waits for my text message to say 'ready', so she can quickly duck over to my place and start the long routine with me. What Stacey might not know is that seeing her face every night – so consistently – has improved my quality of life in leaps and bounds. I've got so many things to worry about in my life, but who's going to put me to bed is not one of them. I don't even consider Stacey a 'carer' anymore, I think of her as my second mum.

I could go on forever about my other carers, like Santiago, who never lets me get away with anything and always challenges my theories on life, or Jasmine, who has to be one of the most efficient people on the planet. But I think they know how much I appreciate them and everything they do for me. At least, I hope they do.

CHAPTER 12
GRATITUDE

*'Learn how to be happy with what you have
while you pursue all you want.'*
– Jim Rohn

Sometimes, I feel like a bit of a prisoner in my own home. There are no bars on the windows, no guards to stop me leaving, but there is an electric gate. It slides along a track on the ground, and that track – only a centimetre high – is enough to stop me. Without help, I can't get over it in my wheelchair. Isn't that wild? A centimetre can be the difference between imprisonment and freedom. But it's not that simple. Even if I could get over that annoying track, beyond it there are cracks in the pavement that could tip my chair, there's a hill that could send me flying, and a whole world that hasn't been built for me.

This probably sounds pretty bleak to you, but over time I've come to appreciate what being stuck – or being still – has taught me. Sitting at my window, I can see people in the street below me rushing around, focused on getting from A to B, always chasing one thing and then another. They never have time to reflect on what they're doing or why they're doing it. And there's so much that they're missing out on. When I'm sitting at my window, I can see the trees blowing softly in the wind, hear the birds chirping or the rain splattering on the roof. I can be totally present and appreciate the small things in life – the things that everyone else is too busy racing past to notice.

We live in a fast-paced world where everyone is always striving for something more. I was one of those people ... once upon a time. I wanted to be picked first, I wanted to make the team, I wanted to win the competition, I wanted to score the game-winning try. And that's not necessarily always a bad thing – that's how you grow, that's how you get better. But when you are always pursuing more, it can be really easy to forget what you have. It can leave you feeling discontent, unfulfilled and unsatisfied.

Life is all about finding that balance between ambition and gratitude. Entrepreneur and author Jim Rohn said it best when he said you have to 'learn to be happy with what you have while you pursue all that you want'. I am all about pursuing greatness – I want to be rich, I want to be successful, I want to be the best I can be – but I make sure I never forget the smaller things or take anything for granted along the way.

So often people fall to one side or the other. Those who are happy with what they've got – and are content with it – may never reach their potential and may never amount to anything substantial. But those who have unrelenting ambition and desire for greatness can often go too far the other way, winding up being greedy, gluttonous and yet still unfulfilled.

Finding the balance between ambition and gratitude is a difficult thing to do, and very few have mastered it. One of my greatest goals in life is to strive for everything I've ever wanted, to achieve everything I possibly can, while at the same time being completely fulfilled and satisfied with what I have. I'm always trying to achieve big things in life and be the best I can be, and I love to travel to the coolest places and eat in fine-dining restaurants. But I'm still completely content with the humble things in life: the sound of stirring a cup of tea, the way a candle lights up my room on a rainy night while I look out my window to the moon, and how the sun shines on me through the car window when I'm stuck in traffic.

Some people want to be on a six-figure salary. They tell themselves, 'When I'm making six figures, I'll be happy', and then they arrive at that moment and the happiness is there, but it's temporary. They're happy for a minute, an hour, a day, a week, or maybe even a year. But eventually, they will get used to having those six figures and that will no longer provide them with happiness. Soon enough they're looking for the next hit.

So they raise the stakes. 'All right, if I can just get to $200,000, then I will be happy.' They reach that goal, and look for the next, raising the stakes again. Constantly striving, chasing happiness; the cycle repeats. Pursuing happiness never actually achieves happiness; all it does is give a temporary feeling of satisfaction that never lasts. This theory is known as hedonic adaptation.

It's not just about money or goals. So often, people decide whether they're feeling good or not based on their external circumstances; their emotions correlate directly to the situation they're in. Someone compliments them, they feel happy; someone insults them, they feel upset. It's the weekend, they're feeling good; it's the work week, they're feeling bad. The situation changes and their emotions do too, because they're chasing happiness externally rather than finding peace internally.

The problem with relying on the good times to give you happiness is that you're putting yourself at risk of losing it in an instant. Sometimes you won't win, sometimes people will put you down, sometimes big issues will arise at work, sometimes you'll get sick. Things don't always go your way, trust me.

The truth is, we're living through a global pandemic, there are wars and humanitarian crises raging in the world, and my home state of New South Wales has been ravaged by fires and floods in recent years. A large part of living isn't sunshine and rainbows, and if your happiness is dependent on everything being good all the time, you're going to be unhappy pretty often.

After my accident, I found myself in a situation where a lot of things had changed in the worst possible way. So I needed to create an equilibrium within myself that would be untouchable and not dependent on any external circumstances.

I FIGHT, YOU FIGHT

I needed to find peace. The pursuit of happiness is not the way to peace. While happiness was always a thing to be chased, peace was something I could call on at any time of day. When you chase happiness, there are highs, and with highs come lows. Peace, on the other hand, is a constant level feeling. That's where I started to turn my attention. Maintaining a constant state of peace meant I wasn't fazed by the regular ups and downs of life, or even being in hospital, or having to learn to live with a catastrophic injury. I learned to control my emotions and find a place of serenity in my mind.

Peace allows me to approach challenges in life with rationality and clarity because it prevents those negative emotions entering and clouding my judgement. So, whenever I come across a difficult obstacle in life, I know what I need to do, and how I am going to do it – one step at a time.

I'm often asked how I feel about the player who tackled me that day. It's not something I love to talk about, and I went back and forth about whether to include it here, but ultimately my answer is: I forgive him completely . . . and it has nothing to do with the fact he brought me a hash brown when he visited me in hospital.

Peace isn't born from a place of victimhood. To have a victim mindset is to be passive, to be overpowered by the emotions created by your circumstances. Sure, we have no control over the circumstances, but we have control over how we respond to them. I have chosen forgiveness and acceptance because I prioritise my peace. I see no benefit in dwelling on the would-haves, should-haves, could-haves. I've learned that, as American basketball coach John Wooden once said, 'things turn out best for the people who make the best of how things turn out.'

At the start of this book, I quoted an old Greek proverb, 'You don't know the true value of water until the well runs dry'. But what I have learned over the years is that if you can do the opposite of this and teach yourself to appreciate the water before the well does run dry, then you will find yourself on a road to peace. And that road is paved with gratitude. Gratitude is a bit of a buzzword at the moment, but it's truly one of the things that got me through what could have been the worst few months of my life. To find a place of peace, I didn't need to cut anything from my life and I didn't need to add anything either. I just needed to implement gratitude.

Happiness occurs when a particular thing meets or exceeds your expectations and desires. But what I soon realised was that you don't need to attain more in order to find happiness – you can find it by simply lowering your expectations and desires so that circumstances more frequently meet and exceed them. Gratitude enables this because it helps you appreciate what you already have – the smaller things, the everyday things – which in turn allows you to find happiness more easily and maintain a more consistent sense of joy.

I FIGHT, YOU FIGHT

And gratitude is important not only when things are going well, but also when you're at your lowest. Anyone can be grateful when they're on a boat in Ibiza, of course, when it's a sunny day and you're listening to their favourite tunes, swimming and eating and celebrating with your best mates. Anyone can be grateful when they're at a restaurant with their family and beautiful hot food gets delivered straight to their table. Anyone can be happy after they've aced an exam or won the big game; the one they've been training for all year.

Who wouldn't be grateful in those moments?

But gratitude is the first thing to be chucked aside when things go wrong. Funnily enough, though, the true benefit of the practice comes when you're able to find gratitude in the worst times; when you are feeling down and upset, when everything seems to be going wrong at work, when you get sick or injured . . . or when you wake up as a quadriplegic.

These moments of difficulty are when the power of gratitude is truly unlocked. I had a certain thing happen to me, but everyone has their own spectrum of what they consider to be challenging things that have happened to them. The key is to stop focusing on what you don't have and start focusing on what you do have. The key is to stop focusing on what is wrong and start focusing on everything that is right. And the most important thing is to find gratitude during those challenging times.

I wasn't always able to do this. Before the accident, when things didn't go my way, I usually did the opposite. When I missed out on a game because I was slightly injured, when I lost a match, or when someone brought me down, I would have a meltdown. Like most teenagers, I would scream or cry or throw a few F-bombs around over the smallest thing my mum or dad said that I didn't agree with. I would either sulk or swear my head off – that was how I dealt with things not going my way. And I don't think I was ever really grateful for all the awesome things I had in my life on an everyday basis – I was only ever grateful for the bigger wins: the compliments from girls, the sports trophies, beating my brothers or my mates in a game (because everyone likes to win!). But all of these things are momentary – they don't stay with you very long, and before you know it, you are no longer grateful; you are no longer satisfied, fulfilled and happy.

I started to find a practice that helped me achieve peace. Five or six times a day, I stopped myself doing whatever I was doing and took a moment to say 'thanks'. I still do it to this day, especially when times get tough and it seems like everything is going against me. Being grateful always brings me straight back to the present moment and reminds me of all of the reasons I have to be happy and to keep fighting. It buoys me right back to that state of peace.

I think when you first start practising gratitude, it has to be a conscious thing – you have to consciously put in the effort and time to really try to find the positive in a situation. But in my experience, if you are consistent with it for long enough, finding gratitude in all sorts of situations can become subconscious and second nature.

To practice gratitude, you can thank God, or the universe, or your dog, or whoever and whatever you believe in. Just rattle off the good things, whatever comes to mind, and be amazed at how your mindset and mood can shift. Start big – your friends, your family, your home, being alive. But get smaller too: I'm grateful for having clean drinking water. I'm grateful I can even swallow water! I'm grateful for the ability to move my arm. I'm grateful for the ability to move my arm and lift my bottle of clean drinking water to my mouth. You get the idea. And suddenly there is so much to be thankful for.

When difficult life events do come along, it can be so easy to focus on everything that is going wrong that it blinds you from seeing everything that you still have – challenging life events so often cause us to lose all gratitude, and our happiness goes out the window with it. However, I have found that if you can finesse the ability to find gratitude when life tries to knock you down, you will find peace providing a constant happiness.

One of the most effective ways to find gratitude when things are tough is by using a comparison strategy. They say that comparison is the thief of joy. They say that you should never compare yourself to someone else. But I don't necessarily agree with this concept. I have found that comparison is one of the best ways to find peace and happiness. Let me explain.

One of the most powerful and important things to remember in life is that our situation could always be worse. No matter how difficult a situation is, no matter how unfair it may be, it could always, always be worse. So, when life tries to knock me down and I find myself in a difficult situation, I use my comparison technique. I imagine myself in a situation that is much worse than what I'm dealing with right now. And from this imaginary position, I compare myself with where I actually am currently. Then, my imaginary self can say to my real self: 'I would do anything to be where you are right now', or 'If only I was where you are right now, I would be so happy.' All of a sudden, I'm no longer down or upset in the difficult situation, I'm grateful and appreciative, bringing me back to peace.

For example, when my mates are all outdoors playing golf or going to the beach together, doing activities that I once loved so much while I have to sit at home by myself feeling left out, it would be so easy to just feel sorry for myself; to curse my disability, to wish I never got injured, to wish I could have my old life back so I was out there with them. But instead of feeling sorry for myself, I reframe my perspective and compare my situation to that period back in ICU when I couldn't even breathe or move a single muscle. Immediately, that so-called 'difficult situation' at home alone doesn't actually seem that bad. In fact, being able to breathe on my own, being able to speak, being able to sit upright in my chair and move around, being able to eat and drink, being at home where I am safe and comfortable . . . it suddenly seems pretty glorious! Simply by reframing my thoughts, I am able to turn a difficult situation into an awesome situation.

Another gratitude technique I often find myself using to maintain my state of peace when things get tough is to look right into the future. I imagine myself when I am in my twilight years – old, sick and dying. I know that when that time comes, I will wish I was exactly where I am today – young, healthy, full of energy and surrounded by loved ones with a whole life ahead of me. Being constantly aware that one day it will all be gone makes me really appreciate the present and what I have . . . while I have it. It makes me appreciate now, live now, laugh now and love now. I think one of the worst things that could happen in life would be getting to the end of it and only then appreciating what we once had – when it's too late.

So, because we could always be in a worse situation in life, we can implement this comparison strategy wherever we are and no matter what challenge we are facing. This way, we will always be able to find joy and happiness, even at the worst of times.

When I wake up in the morning and I can't just get up, I don't focus on the fact that I'm stuck in bed. Instead, I find gratitude and realise how lucky I am to have someone coming to help me, a carer whose work is fully funded by our government. When I remember I have to use a wheelchair for the rest of my life, I don't focus on being stuck in a wheelchair, I find gratitude and realise how lucky I am that I don't have a pressure sore, that I don't have to stay in bed all day or week or year. I don't *have* to use a wheelchair, I *get* to use a wheelchair and continue to live my life.

So, next time you feel like complaining that you *had* to wake up at 6 am, remember that you *got* to wake up at 6 am — because there's no guarantee that anyone will wake up in the morning. No one knows when their last day is going to be. So when I go to bed, I never assume that I will wake up in the morning. I hope I will and I pray I will, but I never assume I will. And every morning when I do wake up, when I open my eyes, I immediately get a sense of relief, I get a slight rush of euphoria and I say to myself, '*Thank you, Jesus*'.

I didn't *have* to wake up at 5.30 am, I *got* to wake up at 5.30 am. Just like that, a simple change in mindset, and I am excited to face the day.

I know a lot of people probably couldn't imagine waking up one day in a wheelchair and feeling grateful for it. I also know that a lot of people couldn't think of a situation that could be worse than waking up in a wheelchair. But trust me it could always be worse, and when I think of that possible outcome, I realise how grateful I am for my life as it is right now.

Most of you reading this could probably leave the house right now and run around the local park if you wanted to. You could run laps, kick a ball, or throw a stick for your dog . . . I can't do that. But I bet when I'm at the park I appreciate it more than you do. I sit there in my chair and I feel the sun shining on my skin, I notice the laughter of the kids nearby, I notice the dogs chasing each other's tails, I notice the colours of the trees and how they move in the wind.

I had no idea how good my quality of life was before the accident. But I didn't appreciate it; I wasn't grateful for it. And I've come to realise if you have a privileged life but you're not aware of all the good things you've got, your life experience is not really much better off than someone who lives a less privileged life but who appreciates the few things they have.

I reckon the true value of our moments in life aren't determined by the quality of them, but by the degree of our appreciation of them. So, I do my very best to appreciate every moment; big and small.

You might not believe me, but in many ways, because of this simple reframing of my thoughts, my life now is better than it was before. I'm awake to all the good things happening around me. So, although my *quality* of life was a million times better before the accident, my life *experience* is now a million times better after the accident. And that is the power of our minds. Happiness doesn't come from *what we have*, it comes from *what we think of it*. As Roman Emperor Marcus Aurelius once said, 'Very little is needed to make a happy life; it is all within yourself, in your way of thinking.'

It's not what we have, it's what we think of it.

But let me give you an example of just how much things have changed for me. Before my accident, I went to the beach all the time. Every single summer from Year 7 to Year 10, you could find me up at 7 am, getting on the bus to Circular Quay. I'd make it to Manly Beach by 9 am, and stay there until sunset, hanging out with my mates, swimming, lying in the sun, getting lunch, swimming some more. As you can imagine, I had an epic tan, and my beach bod wasn't bad either. I absolutely loved being in the water. Only, I don't think I knew how much I loved it, how much I lived for it, until I was stuck in hospital for close to a year. Imprisoned, almost, for more than nine months, without ever setting foot on the hot sand, without ever feeling salt water on my skin. Needless to say, after I got out of rehab, I thought about going back to the beach a lot. The problem was, I didn't know *how* to be at the beach with my new body. Would I get some kind of infection from the water? Am I even allowed to go in ocean water? It seemed risky, I didn't know how it was all going to work. So I made a call to my support coordinator, Lee, and told her I had this gnarly idea about getting back to the beach.

I FIGHT, YOU FIGHT

'Oh, you'll be right,' she said. She was surprisingly chill about it, which was not at all what I'd expected. But she'd given me the green light, so my mates and I picked a day. We packed our towels, got in a van with only one idea in our heads, and finally hit the beach. Chinaman's Beach, to be exact. It was a beautiful day, perfect weather. But for some reason I still felt nervous. How in the world is this all going to work? How am I going to get into the water safely? Even if I do make it to the water, how am I going to stay afloat? What about getting back out? Needless to say, I was wigging out.

When we got there, my mates carried me onto the sand and sat me down on a towel. I was pretty stoked just to be sitting there, but I could tell they wanted to get me into the water.

'C'mon, man. Do it! Get in!' they said.

'Nah, nah, I'll just sit for a bit,' I said, waving them off. I couldn't explain to them how I felt, how worried I was.

It took a bit more convincing and a twenty-minute discussion about the logistics of the thing, but eventually I took off my shirt, and faced the music. The ocean. My old home. My mate Dylan picked me up and carried me down to the water. And when I first touched that blue, blue ocean, it was one of the most glorious feelings I've ever experienced. Salt water on my skin, in my hair, running over my whole body. After a year without the ocean's caress, it felt out of this world, absolutely amazing.

My mates were almost as stoked on my swim as I was. There were eight of them there that day, mates from footy and from school, and we all just chilled in the water, soaking up the magic. I floated on my back for a while with mates taking turns to hold my head up, as I got used to the sensation and letting the sun warm my face. It was complete and total bliss. I never thought I could appreciate the simple pleasure of being in the water on a sunny day with my mates as much as I did.

When I got home that night, I told my mum that I'd been to the beach for the first time since the accident. Before I'd even finished telling her how awesome it had been, how amazing it had felt, she started to cry. She was so happy for me, so stoked. But then she said, 'Thank God you don't tell me about the things you do before you do them!' I laughed. I guess we both had things to be thankful for.

It took losing the ability to walk to realise how precious a few moments floating in the ocean, with the sun on my face and my mates splashing around me, could really be.

There's an analogy I like to remind myself of called 'The Billionaire and the Poor Kid'. The billionaire is eating out at a Michelin-starred restaurant where he orders a $500 steak done 'medium rare'. But he's disappointed and angry when it arrives cooked 'medium' instead. The billionaire's day is ruined, he wants to speak to the manager, he goes home in a rage and tells everyone he knows how hopeless the restaurant is and never to go there. But now imagine the poor kid, who hasn't had a decent meal in weeks, and he gets given just a tiny corner of overdone steak. That kid is over the moon, counting their blessings for weeks. They appreciate what they have, instead of dwelling on what they don't.

I'd rather be the poor kid. And I guess in some ways, I am. Because I'm grateful for the humble things I still have in life. I don't need much to be happy.

Being grateful – particularly in the face of adversity – isn't always the easiest thing to do. It takes a bit of practice, but my challenge to you is the next time something doesn't go your way, before you take any other action, before you have a meltdown, take a moment to reframe, and find gratitude within that difficulty by comparing your situation to one that is worse off. Start there and build on that.

CHAPTER 13
ADAPTATION

'We cannot direct the wind, but we can adjust the sails.'
– Anonymous

Mum screamed and burst into tears when she saw my HSC result. I wasn't even supposed to have graduated. And no, they were not tears of disappointment, or even of relief that I had scraped a pass – they were tears of joy. When I saw that number on the screen, I could hardly believe what I had done.

It had taken everything I had in me to get to this point. And my god it was hard.

I had responded to my injury with a massive pivot. When I was forced to accept that I wasn't going to have a career in rugby, I knew I needed to figure out how to dominate the world in some other way. If I couldn't physically be my best, I wanted to mentally be my best. So, I changed the way I approached school, and my friends noticed. One by one throughout Year 11 they had started to join me up the front of the classroom, leaving our usual back row seats behind us . . . literally.

I had returned to school before I'd returned home. Mum, being a teacher, knew there was no time to waste and wanted to get me back into my studies as quickly as possible. I thought she was crazy, but by February 2019 I'd had my first day back at school as a Year 11 student, if only in a part-time capacity.

Mum had taken the reins on this process, scheduling countless meetings with my teachers to figure out the logistics of me going back to school. We started with PDHPE (Personal Development, Health and Physical Education), where my teacher began by sending me worksheets and homework to complete in hospital. Eventually I was assigned a PDHPE tutor who would come in and help me with the remote work. One tutor soon became two when I picked up my English studies again on top of that.

Next, the school arranged for a robot called 'Milton' to sit in on my classes on my behalf. It was like those robots students started using during the COVID-19 pandemic, which had a camera live streaming the class back to my laptop in rehab. It might sound cool, but I hated it. I remember thinking, *What, I've been demoted to a robot now? I'm not even a human anymore.* The connection felt forced. It only lasted a week. But looking back, I can see how many people were rooting for me; and how badly they wanted to see me succeed that they would even go to the extent of purchasing an expensive robot to sit in classes for me.

My first 'day' back at school, I was only there for two hours. We eased into it with just two periods a week. Fatigue was still a massive issue for me at that point. Mum used to say, 'It doesn't matter how slow we start, it doesn't matter how long it takes, as long as we just get started', and I am so grateful for that. It took about a year to be back at school full time. I remember being so nervous when I rolled through the front gates for the first time again, having weathered a storm most people could only dream of. It was like how I imagine it would feel on your first day of kindergarten, but the difference was that now I was old enough to understand the emotions that came with it.

I worried I would be misunderstood. I was concerned people wouldn't be able to relate to the seismic life event I was still living and experiencing right in front of them. I thought people would treat me differently; that they would think my injury was the ultimate fall from grace . . . From promising rugby star to quadriplegic.

But what I soon came to realise was that I was going to be okay. By the end of the first day, I can confidently say I had never been more popular; I'd never been approached by so many people offering positive reinforcement, support and friendly conversation in a single day.

Despite the whole school being completely wheelchair friendly with elevators and ramps everywhere, of course the *only* place I couldn't get to on the whole campus was where my mates sat for lunch; up two small steps. But we rectified that situation pretty quickly with a makeshift ramp.

Class time was different now too, not only because I sat up front, but because I had a scribe in most subjects as I couldn't write. Having to verbally articulate my words rather than simply writing them straight down on paper was another huge challenge and setback for me. Ninety per cent of the time what the scribe wrote down was nowhere near what I actually wanted to be written down. So, my notes were pretty much someone else's notes that I had to go home and try to understand. I don't know about you, but when I try to read and understand someone else's notes it takes a whole lot longer for the information to sink in than it does when reading my own notes, that have been customised to my brain. As I started to get into the rhythm of the workload and expectations of Year 11, and found that my weekends were now free from both rugby games and detentions, I realised I could dedicate more time to my studies. It was as though the motivation I used to apply to playing rugby was somehow being channelled into other areas. I knew I had it in me to apply myself – I had been doing it my whole life with rugby. But before the accident, I had just never applied myself to anything besides sport.

I had fallen about a year behind in most of my subjects, and the school wanted me to take a couple of extra years to finish Year 12, so I could sit my final exams on an even playing field. But the idea of watching my year group graduate without me – and go on to get jobs, make money and get ahead in life – didn't sit well with me. I wasn't going to fall behind in life, I wasn't going to settle for less.

So, in short, I hustled.

In a typical day as a Year 12 student, I would get picked up at 8 am by a transfer that would get me to school at

8.30 am. But in order to be ready to be picked up at 8, I needed to be up at 5.30 am. That would allow time for the usual things – going to the bathroom, showering and getting dressed – but I also had to account for twenty minutes of what I call 'stands' – practising the movement of standing up and down from the end of my bed with the assistance of a carer holding my wrists and keeping me balanced. Squatting, basically. Up and down for twenty minutes until the alarm goes off on my Alexa . . . plus a few extra minutes usually.

When school finished at 3.30 pm, every day I'd go straight to the gym in Artarmon or physio in Ryde until 6 pm. Once that finished I'd head home to study from 6.30 pm to 10 pm until a carer arrived for my nightly bedtime routine, which could take an hour and a half or more. The aim was to be asleep by 11.30 pm to allow me six hours of sleep. Any more and I felt like it was a waste of precious time I could have been using for something more productive. Any less and my brain wasn't functioning optimally like I needed it to be.

I was using an Apple MacBook by this point, but it didn't have dictation software, so when I was on my own without a scribe, I would study by dictating notes or draft essays on my phone or iPad, which would then connect to my laptop via Google Drive. Not being able to type and having to use dictation was a pretty significant hurdle because it was never seamless; there were always edits arising from the microphone picking up the wrong words, misspelling words (especially nouns!), or just simply not hearing me at all. When I went back to fix the mistakes, I had to do that with my voice too. I would end up sitting there verbally abusing my microphone.

'Go back three letters . . . backspace . . . backspace one, not two! . . . Cap "the" ... no, not *cut* "the", CAP "the". Not cut, CAP!' I would work at the pace of a snail.

In studying terms, a task that might take someone fifteen minutes to do would take me forty-five.

I also had to learn how to be more thoughtful and articulate with my words. As anyone who's written a formal essay would know, you have to use a certain type of language which is pretty dissimilar to the spoken word. I had to dictate in that language, and unlike typing on a laptop where you can delete and rewrite a sentence a few times until it sounds right, I had to fully formulate each sentence before I began.

I had to try overcome these barriers and adapt to this new way of learning as fast as I could so I didn't fall even further behind the rest of my grade. However, no matter how much dictation practice you do, nothing is quite as efficient as typing. Not being able to write and type still inhibits me today as I continue to practice and learn how to effectively verbalise my thoughts using dictation.

As most people would agree, most exams require memorisation of content previously taught and learned. But I couldn't write things down over and over again the way most of my classmates could – I had to memorise everything in the spoken word. I had six subjects – advanced English, business, biology, PDHPE, religion and general maths. Maths was a huge struggle as I couldn't even use a calculator; I had to learn how to calculate most maths problems in my head. I dictated and printed syllabus notes for each subject, and then I laminated them and hung them on my wall next to my bed. Every night, I would read and then look away from my notes for one subject at a time, speaking them out loud and testing my ability to memorise the content. I ended up going over my notes so many times I would start dreaming (or more like having nightmares) about them!

Hustling isn't glamorous, it isn't something I wanted to do. I hated waking up before the sun came up to fit in my 'stands' before school. There were hundreds of things I would have preferred to do besides studying late into the night, six or seven times a week, when the rest of my family were downstairs on the couch watching TV or snuggled up in bed, or – even worse – when all my friends were out on Saturday night at a party. But that's the point: the greatest things in life are the hardest to attain; the difficulty is what gives them value. The most extraordinary things lie at the end of the most challenging paths. If the path was easy, everyone would take it, everyone would make it to the end and the destination would no longer be of significance.

I knew that if I was going to graduate at the same time as my friends and year group, it would be difficult and challenging. And I knew that getting good results on top of that was going to be near impossible. But I wasn't too keen on settling for less than others, and I wasn't really planning on being ordinary either. So, I steered away from the easy path and headed straight down the most challenging path I could find. Along the way I adapted, I dug deep, I sacrificed – and after a sickening amount of hard work, I arrived at my destination.

In November 2020, I managed to graduate Year 12 with my friends and year group. I received a final score of 96.7 and I placed third in the state for PDHPE. And remember Mr McAllan? The teacher who gave me a zero and detention for plagiarising a history assignment in Year 7? He was the same teacher who awarded me a gold certificate for application to studies in every one of my subjects.

And the moment I saw the score on my phone screen, I lifted my head up, leaned back on my chair, and smiled. I took a deep breath and let it out in a sigh of relief. It was worth it – the lonely nights, the early mornings, the missed parties – the hustle. It was all worth it.

CHAPTER 14
ACCEPTANCE

*'Every man has two lives, and the second starts
when he realises he has just one.'*
– Confucius

Becoming a quadriplegic has meant that I face many significant challenges every day of my life – challenges which extend far beyond just the inability to walk, challenges that no one can see. But of all of those challenges I face, there's one that has always stood out. It's something that echoes around my head all day and keeps me up late at night.

When I got injured, I quickly came to notice just how little my body was moving around; how sedentary I was 24/7. I knew that not being able to walk or run around and not having the muscular strength to exercise properly meant that there was very little I could do to maintain things like my cardiovascular health and bone density. To put it simply, I could no longer take for granted the good health I once had.

And so, ever since the accident, I have always had this thought that I would have a shorter life expectancy than the average person. That I would die before my friends. That I would die before my brothers. That I might even die before my parents.

And I know what you're probably thinking – everyone's afraid of dying. I remember when I was in about Year 3, I was staying at my grandparents' house in Townsville and I was lying in bed one night bawling my eyes out. Why? I was in deep thought about what happens to us after we die. Where do we go? What do we do? These thoughts continuously ran through my head. I started freaking out and I realised that once we pass away, that is it, we're gone – erased from the planet forever. Nothing to feel, nothing to think, nothing to look at. Just blank. Just darkness. I continued to cry. I was so scared of dying. But after the accident happened, I wasn't just scared of dying. I was scared of dying young.

Just like I never specifically asked my doctors about my quadriplegic diagnosis, I never asked them about my life expectancy either. I thought about it often, but I was too scared to find out the answer. Scared that I might be right.

But one day – about three years after I was injured – I was sitting at my desk with the Google browser open. I stared at it, contemplating whether or not I should finally find the answer to the question that had plagued my thoughts nearly every day since the accident.

I typed in the question a few times, always deleting it before I hit enter. But after an internal tug of war that lasted about half an hour, I worked up the courage to type it in: *What is the life expectancy of a quadriplegic, aged 16?"*

I braced myself for the results, praying to God that my fears wouldn't be realised.

The top result read: *The life expectancy of a quadriplegic, injured at age 16, is 50 years – 33.2 years less than the average male.*

I was right.

I FIGHT, YOU FIGHT

I waited for the tears. I waited for the wash of pain and sadness. But . . . they didn't come. The words on the screen didn't traumatise me, didn't get me down, didn't imprison me. I didn't sit there and cry and give up. Instead, the exact opposite happened. In that very moment, my entire life changed. I became completely liberated. In learning about my own death, I learned to live – and I figured out exactly how I wanted to do it. I knew, in that moment, that I'd rather spend forty years on Earth lived to the absolute fullest than eighty years tiptoeing through life trying to make it to the end comfortably and safely.

Nowadays, it's not death that I'm afraid of. It's not the thought of dying young that scares me either. Rather, it's the thought of getting to the end of my life and realising that I could have done more. Realising that I could have been more. Realising that I had untapped potential. Realising that I lived a life that was less than the one I was capable of living. Dying doesn't scare me, but not reaching my full potential absolutely terrifies me.

So the question I needed to ask myself became: *How can I possibly reach my potential when I have such a short time to live?*

I've now come to terms with the fact that death will come for me sooner than most. I've come to terms with the fact that most of the people I love will probably outlive me. They know who they are and I hope they don't cry when they read this.

This isn't something I have spoken about openly with anyone before. But I'm ready to talk about it now, because knowing that I may die young has been one of the best things that has ever happened to me – it has taught me how to live. Properly. It has taught me three of the most valuable lessons I have ever learned about how to live a fulfilled life. The lessons are: accept what you can't control, embrace discomfort and vulnerability, and be disciplined.

I learned that first lesson – about accepting the things you can't control – when I woke up in ICU. But I don't think the true power of the lesson ever really hit me until the day I sat at home on my computer and confronted my worst fears about my own mortality. I received the worst possible news, and all I could do was accept it. But that acceptance freed me from grief and propelled me forward.

When things happen to us, of course our immediate response is to try to fix the problem and find a solution. But in life, things happen to us that we have no control over. There are some things that we just cannot change. When these things happen, we are left with two simple options. We can accept it for what it is and move on, or we can choose the easier option; to hold on to what has hurt us and waste time wishing that it didn't happen.

Knowing that my time here on this planet is already limited, I realised I had no time to waste on grieving and wishing. Because doing so would only bring me a life of misery and feeling sorry for myself, a life of anger and unhappiness. A life that may not even be worth living.

So in that moment, despite the emotional pain I was going through, I knew that I just had to accept it and find a way to carry on in order to live my life while I had the chance.

Refusing to accept the things you can't control in life is, simply put, time-wasting and energy-sucking. And because I have less time than the average person, I am quick to jump off any merry-go-round that isn't taking me to where I want to go. I will always accept any situation exactly as it is, move on if it isn't serving me, and pivot towards something that will.

There's a photo I love of this tree which demonstrates this first lesson. It looks like it has been chopped down, the trunk lying on the ground. Yet, despite that, tree branches are still visible, growing upright from the trunk, along the entire length of it. It's sort of like a sideways tree. I can hear you asking, 'Where are you going with this, Alex?', and to that I'd say, I reckon this photo is a pretty accurate visual representation of the world we live in – the universe doesn't care about what you've gone through to get something, only about whether you get there or not. The world doesn't care how unfair our lives are compared to the lives of others, or how many more challenges we face than someone else. All that matters is whether or not we get to where we're trying to go.

So, when we come across obstacles and challenges in our lives that we can't change, no matter how unfair they are, we've just got to accept that they are there and find a way to carry on, just like that sideways tree.

CHAPTER 15
VULNERABILITY

*'It is not death that you should fear,
but never beginning to live.'*
– Marcus Aurelius

Learning that my time here on this planet will likely be shorter than everyone else's made me realise just how important it was to make the most of the time I do have. It made me realise that I would need to push myself, to grow faster, learn quicker, and work harder to achieve my goals and live the fullest life I am capable of.

When I challenge myself to think about times in my life when I've grown the most, when I've felt like I was living life to the fullest, it's always a moment when I was in an uncomfortable situation. So, this was the next lesson for me – and it was all about how discomfort and vulnerability can create the best environment for personal growth, expansion and success.

Discomfort and vulnerability have underpinned nearly every single memory I have where I could confidently say I was living my best life. So what did that teach me? In order to properly live life to the fullest, I have to totally embrace those feelings of fear and lean into them. I have to leave my comfort zone – get uncomfortable and get vulnerable – in order to grow.

About six months after I left the rehab centre, an opportunity came my way that put me just about as far out of my comfort zone as it was possible to go. Two ladies showed up at our house after requesting a meeting with Mum and me through our *I Fight You Fight* channels. They introduced themselves as Angie Farr-Jones and Jeanine Treharne, and gave us an introduction to the organisation they worked for, called Stand Tall.

Stand Tall, they told us, brings stories of hope and courage to young people – aiming to improve their mindsets and ultimately the course of their lives. It was the first time I'd ever heard of this organisation, and I was intrigued, but also a little confused as to why they were telling me about it at all – until they asked me if I would like to speak at one of their student events . . .

My stomach turned at the mention of it. I hated public speaking. Does anyone actually like it? I hated the idea of everyone staring at me, I hated the idea of screwing up and embarrassing myself. I didn't even like the idea of telling my story out loud at that point, even if it could potentially help others.

The first thing I said was, 'How many people would it be in front of?', expecting the answer to be somewhere in the ballpark of 100–150 students.

'Six thousand students,' Angie replied.

Picking up my jaw from the floor, I couldn't even reply.

Jeanine, clearly not reading the room, added 'Well, six thousand *in person*, and about 100,000 joining online from across the country.'

I FIGHT, YOU FIGHT

What the?! The closest thing I could remember doing that felt like a 'big speech' was presenting to my grade in Year 4; which was about 50 people!

Are they giving me a choice here? I wondered. Because if they were, the easy answer was definitely, 'Thanks, but no thanks.' Why would I want to put myself through that? And then I thought about it a little bit more, and asked myself: *Why am I saying no? Because it would make me uncomfortable? Because I'd feel nervous? Isn't that a reason* to *do it?*

I realised that if I was so hell-bent on achieving big things in this lifetime, then I needed to get out of my comfort zone and say yes to opportunities like this. And wasn't sharing my message with an audience of 106,000 a pretty big thing?

So, knowing I'd be nervous, knowing I'd be vulnerable, knowing that I could completely embarrass myself, knowing that I'd much prefer not to do it, I said yes.

Fast forward four months, to June 2021, and it was one of my first ever public talks, at the International Convention & Exhibition Centre in Sydney's Darling Harbour. Just as Jeanine had promised, there were 6,000 people in the auditorium and 100,000 online. I didn't sleep much the night before, but it's probably no shock to anyone that I woke up nice and early on the day of the talk. I was working with some social media managers who came over beforehand to help me prepare. We did a few run-throughs and they gave me a few tips about presenting, telling me that a successful speech is 20 per cent content, and 80 percent your delivery on the day. So, no pressure.

Once we arrived at the centre I wove through crowds of people. People who were all there to listen to *me*. I was introduced to another presenter, Michael Crossland, an elite businessman who survived life-threatening cancer *and* a horrific cancer drug trial. I made a point to sit in the audience for his talk, though I don't know if that was a great idea. I watched him in awe as he owned the stage for an hour with no notes. I clutched my notes even tighter in my lap.

Eventually I was ushered backstage, where I was told to wait in the wings until the speaker before me finished and I was introduced by the master of ceremonies. Feeling the nerves and wishing I didn't have to roll out there, I reminded myself that I wasn't doing this for me – I was doing it for everyone out there in the audience. I decided nerves were a purely selfish feeling, born from thoughts about how I could embarrass myself or stuff up. But this wasn't about me. It was about something so much bigger than me. And when I say bigger, I mean 106,000 people bigger.

The spotlights were warm on my face and my arms were shaky as I rolled across to the centre of the stage, but as soon as I opened my mouth and said my first words, the nervous tension fell away and I gained an awesome sense of clarity. I felt comfortable. I guess it's true what Muhammad Ali once said: it's not the mountains ahead of you that wear you out, it's the pebble in your shoe. It's the thoughts you tell yourself. It's the mental game.

I received a standing ovation that day and saw tears in the eyes of a few audience members. I was on a high afterwards and started seeking out more opportunities to share my story. To this day, I still don't think there's a better feeling than finishing one of my presentations and knowing I've gotten through to the audience, and hearing feedback like, 'You inspired me', 'You changed me', 'You helped me'.

Every time I am asked to speak in an event, I know that I'm going to be uncomfortable and nervous, I know that I could easily forget my lines, embarrass myself and fail, I know that I'd much prefer to take the easy route in life, stay in my comfort zone and say 'no' ... But I embrace my discomfort and vulnerabilities and say 'yes' to every speaking opportunity. By doing so, I am able to live to my fullest – making a positive impact on the world and leaving behind a legacy.

I know it would be easier to stay on the couch with a cup of tea, wrapped up in a cosy blanket (or cotton wool), watching a movie in the safety and comfort of my own home. But there is no potential to be reached from there. There is no growing to be done from the couch.

That's also why in 2022 I decided to book a trip to Europe. With my mates, and in a chair.

Chasing a European summer in the mid-year uni break is a rite of passage for many Australian eighteen-year-olds, and

I was no exception. And while it sounds glamorous – and *is* glamorous for so many travellers – for me the four weeks of the trip were up there with some of the hardest weeks of my life, even if they were also some of the most rewarding.

The main reason I wanted to go? FOMO, Fear of Missing Out. It started with my brother Zac. I remember him lying on the couch one day talking about an epic Euro-trip he was planning, rattling off the names of exciting sites and cities he was going to visit, and it didn't take long until I joined in on the conversation. But while I loved the idea of travel, going to Europe still wasn't a realistic option for me. A few more weeks passed and more mates started talking about a trip. My FOMO got so bad I eventually asked myself the question, *Why couldn't I go?* And once I asked that question, it became way more than just FOMO, it became: *Why should I let this chair hold me back from doing something I want to do?*

I knew it was going to take extra work to plan a wheelchair-friendly trip, so once my mate Dylan was on board, I did most of the heavy lifting, making sure our itinerary was completely accessible. I carried a sort of guilt that it was going to be harder work for him travelling with a disabled friend, and I wanted to make the trip as seamless as possible for him. I used to joke to Mum that I was going to need another holiday after planning this first holiday because it took so much effort. But planning a wheelchair-friendly trip through a number of non-English-speaking countries

I FIGHT, YOU FIGHT

on the other side of the world wasn't my only challenge (although making sure each street, hotel, taxi, restaurant and day trip was accessible was pretty bloody hard). The challenges continued the moment I arrived at the airport to leave Sydney.

You get a lot of stares in a wheelchair in an airport . . . and on the plane. You board the plane first, before you're transferred out of your regular wheelchair into an 'aisle chair', which is a specially made wheelchair skinny enough to fit down the aisle of the plane. The other passengers watch on as your mates pick you up and do the transfer. The aisle chair isn't built like your normal wheelchair, it's much more uncomfortable, so you're having to balance yourself in it using your head and neck against the headrest. Your skinny limbs are hanging awkwardly in the most abnormal positions. Your stomach is exposed as your top is gathered under your arms from being lifted between chairs. Your SPC (that's a urine catheter), which is normally discreet and neatly hidden, is poking out. They wheel you down to your seat in the new aisle chair and your knees knock against everyone else's as you go. When you finally get there, the ordeal to get you into your seat means everyone queued behind you to reach their seat has to wait. The other passengers try to be polite – they're showing patience for the poor kid in the wheelchair – while simultaneously just wanting to take their own seats.

Inferior is a good word to describe how it feels. Embarrassing too.

But the enjoyment and growth I get from travelling far outweigh the discomfort I feel doing it, and that's the point. It's a perfect paradox that proves my point that only when we are prepared to feel discomfort and vulnerability are we going to be rewarded with growth and success, and life. The more you fear, the more you grow. The more risks you take, the greater the reward.

Remember Benji's spoon? I took it with me on that first trip. Actually, a few hours before I left for the airport, Mum flagged that I should probably take a *back-up* spoon, in case I lost it (I was always forgetting it at restaurants). So Benji was put back to work. This time, his creation was a spoon with custom finger holes made with zip-ties. It was a good thing I had it, because the original spoon never made it to Europe. I left it on the plane. I also left my laptop on the plane. Unfortunately, Benji hadn't made me a back-up for that. It was going to be fine, right?!

I remember being in Taormina, on the coast of Sicily, and we decided we wanted to go to the beach – after all, it was 38 degrees. We drove to where the map told us we'd find a carpark and arrived there to find it was actually positioned at the top of about 120 seriously steep stairs, which led down to a hidden beach. My mates and I stood at the top, looked down and contemplated the descent. Immediately I said,

I FIGHT, YOU FIGHT

'Nup, sack it!', knowing it would be too hard and too risky. But my mates, being as good as they are, were up for the challenge and wanted to go for it.

Still, I pushed back and wanted to take the easier and safer option – a more accessible beach or simply a pool – where I wasn't vulnerable and at risk of being hurt. We discussed it (okay, we argued) for a couple of minutes until Jayden made a good point when he told me, 'Just imagine this is the sickest beach you have ever seen. You'd regret being so close and not seeing it.' So, I disregarded the discomfort I would face, I embraced my vulnerability and agreed to the plan.

We tossed up whether it would be better to carry me separately to the chair or keep me in my chair and wheel down each step. We decided on option two. I was scared, knowing it would only take one wrong foot on their part and I'd be tumbling down those stairs with no limbs capable of stopping me. But no risk, no reward . . . right?

After a few slips and close calls, we got down the first flight of stairs and changed tack. We realised it would be easier if they carried me and the chair separately. So, Jayden lifted me out and we went for it. Dylan and Santi followed behind with my chair. In Jayden's arms, my head was lolling and my hips were popping in and out of their sockets. The boys were stuffed when we reached the bottom. Totally fatigued. But the reward waiting at the bottom made it all worth it. In front of us was one of the most pristine and beautiful beaches

I've ever laid eyes on. The sand was white and soft and warm. The water was turquoise, clear and shimmering.

On the other side of fear, on the other side of effort, on the other side of discomfort is beauty, bliss, growth, achievement, life. Think of a fish: if a fish plays it safe and never opens its mouth, it'll never get caught by a fishing hook. But it will also never be able to eat and grow and live.

~

Going to the beach for a surf had always been one of my favourite things to do before the accident, but I rarely get to do it post-accident because wheelchairs aren't built for sand, and beaches aren't all that accessible. But on a family trip to the Gold Coast in 2021, I was inspired to try surfing again. For me, the regret I feel after I play it safe by choosing not to do something is always worse than doing it and failing. If I don't do something, I'm always left wondering what it would have been like and where it might have taken me. I think that's what got me back in the water. Better an 'Oh well' than a 'What if?' Though I was definitely expecting it to go more 'Oh well' on this occasion, especially since I'd been told all I needed to be able to do was prop myself up on my elbows, and I couldn't even do that! The entire car ride there, I envisioned myself face down on the surfboard like a penguin sliding along ice.

I remember taking my shirt off on the promenade before being carried down to the water. It was something I used to do with pride, knowing how fit, tanned and built I was. But this was a very different experience, as I found myself feeling self-conscious about baring my skinny and pale body to hundreds of people at the beach. My arms were smaller, my stomach bigger, and I had the addition of my SPC. As if I wasn't feeling vulnerable enough, it took four people from the surf school to lift me from my chair down onto the sand and into the water. I've done some hard things in my life, but putting on the provided rashie was up there. It was the tightest thing I've ever had to squeeze into and the same four people who lifted me onto the sand had to pull my flailing arms and head through it in a group effort that took about ten minutes.

Finally, I was ready to get into the water. But the same salt water that used to bring me so much freedom now filled me with worry. I knew the risks – of course I did. I knew I was risking further injury, I knew I couldn't swim, I knew there would be little hope for me if I took in any water, or got stuck in a position where my breathing was compromised. But I reminded myself: I'm here for a good time, not a long time.

One of the instructors took my board, and my dad and Zac picked me up in a sort of fireman's carry towards the water. They lay me flat on the surfboard. I was stomach down with my face pressed against the Styrofoam as my neck couldn't lift my head, and I couldn't even see what was in front of me. The instructors began pushing my board up and over waves, out past the shore and whitewash. They'd tell me to hold my breath every time a wave came and my board nosedived under it. The movement caused the skin on my face to rub against the board, completely grazing up my chin and nose.

After a little while, they swung my board around to catch the wave – or so they told me – but I still couldn't see anything, and next thing I knew, they were pushing my board and swimming alongside me as an incoming wave took us back to shore. That feeling of gliding, by myself, at speed, along the surface of the water, transported me back in time to a previous life when I was able and fast and free. It was heaven, if only for a moment.

I had just finished school and found myself with a lot more free time during which I started searching for those fleeting moments of freedom in other extreme sports – including kayaking, jet skiing, snorkelling and camel riding – but I don't think I've ever come closer to pure, euphoric freedom than when I was free-falling out of a plane 15,000 feet above the ground.

I didn't always want to skydive – I wasn't one of those people who have it on their bucket list. But on my new quest to get out of my comfort zone I knew this was probably the holy grail. It just so happened that around the same time a social media organisation called Jack Nimble began chatting to Tess about shooting a promotional video for my 'I Fight,

I FIGHT, YOU FIGHT

You Fight' campaign – and they thought a shot of me skydiving would be just the thing.

During the two weeks before I took the plunge, I couldn't sleep. I was too nervous. Too many things could go wrong. Even for someone who wasn't a quadriplegic, tandem skydiving is literally handing over your life to someone else. They decide when to jump, they pull the ropes, they adjust the parachute. But at least if you're able-bodied you can lift your legs up before you land without risking snapping them. And you might be capable of pulling some emergency string to inflate a parachute in the event that your instructor passes out. These were the types of thoughts running through my head.

The morning of the dive, the boys came over to my place so we could all freak out together. For the entire hour-and-a-half car ride from Gladesville to Wollongong we were choked by trepidation and angst – none of us said much. When we got there, we checked in and did our introductory session, only to find out our jump had been delayed. The delay only exacerbated our anxious thoughts: *Is it too windy? Has there been a problem? Is this God's way of telling us we shouldn't do it?* We sat around some more before they finally took us in for our training session. It felt like a lifetime had passed before we were in the car on our way to the runway.

The plane ride up was the worst part. My body had a physical reaction to the nerves and I got heaps of spasms, causing all my muscles to involuntarily contract. After a five minute ascent, I thought, *All right, surely this is high enough?* Another five minutes and we were still ascending. After about 25 minutes, we were above the clouds – 15,000 feet – and we could no longer see the ground beneath us. When they opened the door, nothing felt real. *Surely we're not going to jump from here?* The wind was streaming into the small plane, blowing back my hair and almost drowning out my own terrified thoughts with its noise.

I was to jump first. I was strapped to the front of an instructor, who pushed me across the small plane to the opening. I had no choice. I don't have control over my body at the best of times, but at this point he was calling all the shots. Once we were almost hanging out of the door, they began a countdown. *Five . . . four . . . three . . . two . . .* I braced myself as best I could.

Then we were falling.

The actor Will Smith has a great YouTube video about his own skydiving experience. He describes the whole thing as a really interesting confrontation with your own fear, because when you're standing there with your toes hanging out the door of a plane, you've never felt so scared, but the moment you jump – the split second the free fall begins – you encounter pure, euphoric bliss. 'The point of maximum danger is the point of minimum fear,' he says.

And falling is the wrong word. It's actually flying.

I FIGHT, YOU FIGHT

I was flying. I was free. I actually screamed the words 'Freedom, baby!' over my shoulder to the instructor as we were streaming through the air, the wind filling out my cheeks. It's amazing to witness your emotions swing like a pendulum from scared half to death to euphoric in a fraction of a moment.

We made it back to solid ground – the parachute didn't malfunction, and my instructor didn't pass out. He had a rope looped around my knees so he could keep my legs out of the way of his landing, which was seamless. I remember noticing the huge smile spreading across my face as my mates landed around me, and Mum and Dad ran towards me cheering.

As Will Smith concludes in his video, 'God placed the best things in life on the other side of fear.'

On the other side of fear is bliss.

Our buzz stayed with us for the rest of the day. That night we celebrated in a hostel in Manly, where we had more filming for the promotional video the next day. We were out until 6 am and up at 7 am for an 8 am shoot.

My experiences with public speaking, travelling and skydiving have taught me that it's important to cultivate a 'What if?' attitude to life. And it's not the kind of 'What if?' you're probably used to. It's not 'What if I fail?' or 'What if things go wrong?'. It's the opposite, it's 'What if I succeed?'

I could say no to a public speaking gig, but what if it helps one kid feel happier?

I could hurt myself surfing or skydiving, but what if it's a life-changing experience?

I wake up most days and ask myself: *What if. . . ?*

'What if' plants the idea that your potential has no limits. It dares you dream about what could be possible if you *actually* applied yourself to do your *very* best.

It also helps me confront my own mortality: *I could just lounge around today, but what if . . . this is my last day here on Earth?* – and my answer to that is, well, then I am going to make the absolute most of today and give my absolute best. And when the next day comes around, and the same thought sticks in my head, I ask myself 'What if?' again. This is why I can't sit around the house and do nothing; this why I don't laze on the couch; this why I very rarely watch movies.

These 'What ifs' constantly run around my head and ignite a fire within me – a burning desire to do my very best and reach my full potential every day; to not waste any minute.

There's a saying in footy circles: leave everything out on the field. And while now I don't have footy, per se, I still like to apply this same mindset to my life; the field of life. I plan to give it my all and leave everything out there.

I remember one lunchtime at school in Year 12 when I was sitting and chatting with a couple of my mates, Nick and Harri, while we watched the rest of the boys play footy on Gorman oval just next to the English classrooms. As I was chowing down my chicken salad, a shadow approached us from behind – it was the Deputy of Students, Mr Newman. Never a good sign.

Mr Newman stopped right in front of me, with complete disregard for the conversation we were in the middle of (and the fact I had a mouth full of food), and looked me straight in the eye and said, 'Alex, you should study business and law.'

My first reaction was to laugh, I nearly choked on my food. I replied, 'Ha, there's no way. There's no way I'm doing law. Not in a million years!' Keep in mind that until my final year, my whole schooling life I had been getting passes and rarely ever got over 70 percent. I wasn't even planning on going to university at all. My options were always either become a professional rugby player or – if that didn't work out – become a bricklayer or a sprinkler fitter through TAFE. I remember I had a few meetings with the careers counsellor at school, who gave me a pamphlet about a career in bricklaying which said you can make fifty cents per brick! I did some quick maths and thought that would be pretty good money to make.

Unfortunately, all three of those options were off the table now.

But I still said 'no way' to Mr Newman's suggestion of studying law because I knew would be vulnerable taking subjects with other students who were ten times smarter than me. I knew I'd have to put in extra hours just to keep up with them, and I didn't want to risk failing and embarrassing myself.

Mr Newman replied, 'You know what, Alex, just think about it. Just think about it.'

I disregarded it and went back to my chicken salad. But that night, while I was lying in bed and reflecting on the day, I thought back to that conversation. *Me? A lawyer?* Before long I applied the 'What if?' rule.

What if I could somehow graduate with my year group.

What if I did well enough at school to get into uni?

What if I did study law?

What if I did graduate from uni with a law degree, where could that take me? What could I achieve and how far could I go?

The possibilities made me silly with excitement. These thoughts made me brave enough to embrace my vulnerabilities, embrace the discomfort, and embrace the risk. The very next day I went to Mr Newman's office and I said, 'Whatever, I guess I'll try law.'

I started applying the 'What if?' rule to all of my studies, and to my whole life.

There's this thought experiment I love, which I saw in a video by a Navy SEAL called David Goggins. He asks you to imagine arriving in heaven and being met by God (or whoever you believe in) at the pearly gates. And standing there awaiting your arrival, God's holding a list – it's a list he's going to show you of all the things you could have done, everything you could have been, everything he had planned for you. How does it feel when he shows you the list, and you see all the things that are left unticked? On the other hand, how does it feel seeing everything ticked off – knowing you've done everything you were destined for, knowing you fulfilled your life and potential?

What if studying business and law is on that list? What if becoming a barrister is on that list? What if owning my own business is on that list? What if delivering speeches or writing a book that makes a positive difference is on that list?

When I was holed up in my room studying for ten, twelve or fourteen hours at a time during the week or on the weekend, or when my light was the only one left on in the house because everyone else was asleep while I was still working away, I would ask myself: *What if I just did one extra hour of study, would that be what it takes to get the mark I need?* And even after I'd done that extra hour, the same question constantly came back: *'What if . . . just one more!'*. 'What ifs?' kept coming – there was always more to do. That was all the motivation I needed.

At the end of 2020, I got a letter in the mail that would have made Mr Newman smile. I had been accepted to a business and law degree at the University of Technology Sydney.

People have told me that I am smart because of my marks and because of what I am studying. People have told me that I am a gifted and natural public speaker. But I always tell them the truth: I'm not actually that smart, I'm really not naturally gifted, I just get out of my comfort zone, I get vulnerable, I take risks and I put in the hard, relentless, ugly work.

To achieve those really important and significant goals in life, you have to try things that are new and scary, to take chances and to get uncomfortable. Think about it, when you go after something that is important to you, it's usually a little bit scary: proposing to your partner (*What if they say no?*), going for a promotion (*What if I don't get it?*), or starting up your own company (*What if it fails and I lose a lot of money?*). Those are some terrifying scenarios, but at times like these you need to be asking yourself a very different kind of 'What if?' question: *What if they say yes and we live happily ever after? What if I get the promotion and I can use it to support my family? What if I start up my own company and it becomes the next Apple? What if I completely commit myself to my goal every day, could I become the next Da Vinci or Bill Gates or Lionel Messi?* Asking these kinds of 'What ifs' makes you wonder what your potential is; how far you can go.

And that's the point: our potential is so much greater than we think it is but the limitations of comfort, safety and pleasure stop us from ever getting there. To overcome these limitations and discover our true potential, we need to embrace discomfort, embrace vulnerability, embrace fear, embrace risks and ask the question: *what if?*

CHAPTER 16
DISCIPLINE

'Discipline is choosing between what you want now and what you want most.'
– Anonymous

I hope this book does not motivate you.

Let me explain . . .

A lot of people would probably tell you that I've always been very disciplined, especially with my sport. But the truth is that I was never really disciplined. I was only ever motivated. And motivation only gets you so far.

When it came to rugby, I was always extremely motivated. I would be the first one in the gym, and I would be the last one to leave. I would be the first one on the training oval after school and I would still be on the field doing my own sprint training or goal kicking long after the rest of the team had gone home. I was motivated to be the best rugby player that I could be. I was motivated to make it professional. And I would sacrifice everything in order to reach this dream of mine.

I was motivated to play rugby because I loved to play rugby, because I felt like playing rugby, because it was my dream to play rugby.

But what about things that I didn't want to do? What happened when it came to my studies? What happened when it came to chores? What happened when it came to my relationships? What happened when it came down to helping others?

There was no motivation at all. I had no motivation because I didn't *want* to do these things, because I didn't *feel* like doing these things, because I wasn't *motivated* to do these things. So, whenever it came down to something I didn't *want* to do, I didn't do it – or, if I did do it, it was a complete drag and I did it half-heartedly.

So you see, when you're motivated, you only do things you're supposed to do *because* you're motivated to do those things. You only go to the gym when you're motivated to work out. You only study when you're motivated to learn. You only clean your room when you're motivated to get rid of all the clutter.

But motivation comes and goes; it's fleeting. Some days you wake up and you feel horrible. You're tired, or you're sore. You've got a headache, or it's cold outside. You're upset, or sad. You're not motivated. Not all the time. And often you're simply not going to be motivated to do certain things. Things that you should be doing; things that will benefit your life. Motivation only gets you so far in reaching your potential.

What it really takes is discipline. And that was my third lesson.

Discipline is doing what you know you *should* do, not what you *want* to do. Discipline is acting for your future self, not your current self. Discipline is showing up for yourself when you'd rather stay in bed and hide from it all. Discipline is getting up at 5.30 am when you've worked until 1 am the night before. It's sacrificing going out with your mates to finish a project you're working on, or to hit the gym. It's saying 'no' to the sticky date pudding when you're craving it most.

Discipline doesn't take into consideration how you're feeling. It's doing the right thing anyway, despite how you feel. It's choosing the road that the best version of yourself knows it should take, not the one that would bring you fleeting and instant gratification.

Discipline has changed how I approach my life now. Regardless of how I may be feeling on any particular day, I do what I should be doing, not what I want to be doing.

After a long twelve-to-fifteen-hour day of hustle, work and training, one of my carers arrives to help me into bed at about 10 pm. When they arrive, I shut down my laptop, I quietly turn off the final upstairs light and I come downstairs in the elevator feeling completely drained and exhausted from a big day. Its late, and all I want to do is to jump straight into bed, get horizontal and fall asleep. But just when I think it's finally time to relax and rest, I remember that I still need to go through the two hour process of getting into bed, which includes twenty minutes of 'stands', plus my arm exercises. Every night, a voice in my head says to me: *'Sack the exercise and just go to bed!'*, or *'Have a night off, Alex, you deserve it'*, or *'You're too tired, go to sleep'*. But, every night, there I am on the edge of my bed – squatting up and down, up and down. Not because I want to, but because the future me will wish that I did.

Once my head finally hits that pillow (and after a sigh of relief that could wake up my neighbours), I use Siri to text my morning carer to let them know when to come and help me out of bed. And each time I go to tell Siri a time, there is nothing I want more than to say, '10 am please' and have a fat sleep-in. Because I absolutely *love* sleep. Especially during winter, when the sheets are up around my face and I'm cosy and warm. Yet every single morning the text message ends up being, '5.30 am please' or '6 am please'. Every morning, I'm up before dawn. Before the birds start chirping. Before the morning ruckus of my family. It's me, on my shower chair, in the cold, in the dark, tired, groggy and alone.

Even though I'm up before everyone else, I still end up hearing my family begin their days before me. They get on with their lives, ticking off their tasks while I fall behind, stuck in my tedious and time-consuming morning routine. I know I could play the victim card and say, 'Well, the game of life is rigged against me, so why even try to compete with others when I'm already at such a disadvantage?' I think I'm speaking not just for myself, but for other people in my situation, when I say that I don't want to settle for a life that is 'less' than that of the average person. And I don't want to settle for a life that is mediocre either. I refuse to compare myself to the average Joe and just compete with normal people; I want to be extraordinary, I want to really leave a mark on this world.

I FIGHT, YOU FIGHT

So, I have to wake up earlier than everyone, go to bed later than everyone and work twice as hard as everyone. That's why when my carer quietly knocks on my bedroom door, I fling my sheets off, tell Alexa to turn my lights on, and I say to them, 'Let's do this!' And what I mean is: Let's pump out the morning routine so I can go hustle, get out there and achieve my goals. So that I can make the most of today and, in the end, my life.

Your emotions do not always have your best interests at heart. Your emotions will tell you it's far nicer to sleep in. They'll cloud your judgement. They'll challenge what you know is best for you. And what I've learned is that you need to be bigger – to be thinking bigger – than your emotions and what you feel like in any particular given moment. A human's natural instinct is to keep themselves safe – that's why your body rejects doing the difficult or challenging thing. It has an internal compass working to keep you out of harm's way. But so often that's not the way you're going to maximise your growth and success as a person.

Comfort is addictive. The few times I did try sleeping in was when I was on holiday in Europe and I had a carer travelling with me full time. Over there, it was far too easy to tell them to give me a few extra hours of sleep when they'd check to see if I was ready to get up at 6 am. It was luxurious and I absolutely loved it; and I reckon I deserved that small reprieve from my usual routine. But when I got back to

Australia and noticed I was tempted by that desire to sleep in again, I reassessed the situation. I saw what it was doing to me. I felt myself getting lazy. I noticed I was cheating myself out of the things that are good for me. If I sleep in, then I don't have the time to practise standing, or squeeze in an extra hour of study, or rehearse an upcoming speech, or answer my emails before I have to be in class.

And more than that, I noticed I was giving in to other desires. I noticed myself stopping work early so I could get on the couch and watch a movie. I was making up excuses to skip gym in the morning. My email inbox was getting fuller and fuller. I was doing fifteen minutes of stands in the morning and night rather than my mandatory twenty. I even noticed myself getting lazy with my usually strict diet and started hitting the carbs.

It's the insignificant habits that are the biggest killers. You might tell yourself, *Ah whatever, it's only one caramel slice*, or *Okay, just fifteen minutes' more sleep*. But really, these little habits have a big effect on who we are as a whole person. They create us, shape us, define us.

James Clear talks about something similar in his book, *Atomic Habits*. He talks about how the small and seemingly insignificant choices we make every day can add up. Our choices are what comes between who we are and who we could be. Or as Will Durant once said, paraphrasing the philosophy of Aristotle, 'We are what we repeatedly do'.

I FIGHT, YOU FIGHT

And I knew that if I kept letting these small things slide, I would notice my goals begin to slip away from me. Since realising that, I've never deviated from the routine again. Well, almost never.

And speaking of routine, I know I've mentioned my 'standing' exercises a few times so I thought I should explain why I do them. I realise that it's highly unlikely I'll wake up one day and be able to walk again. But I also know the only way there's a chance of that ever happening is if I dedicate this time every day to practising the movement and attempting to build the muscle and neuropathways that might one day make it possible.

Miracles don't happen overnight. Athletes don't become the best in the world without sacrifice and training. People don't make it to the top of Mount Everest without preparation and setbacks. Everyone loves to see the glory, but few are willing to do what it takes to get there. Even if I am never able to walk again unassisted, I know that practising standing will contribute to my strength, fitness, bone density and overall health and will hopefully go towards extending my life expectancy.

So, without fail, whether I'm hungover, sick, sore or weak, I stand up and down for twenty minutes twice a day. Up and down, up and down. Morning and night. Every day, 365 days a year. Boring, repetitive, frustrating. But also: discipline.

Another non-negotiable part of my morning routine is getting to the gym before the rest of my working day starts. As soon as I've finished the stands, I either pump weights, I get on my hand cycle machine and push out 4 km as fast as I can, or I do some boxing. Because I'm not strong enough to really give my cardiovascular system a workout, I try to put more pressure on my body and make it harder for myself by closing my mouth and exclusively breathing through my nose during these exercises. And when my nose is blocked? New difficulty level unlocked!

One of the hardest things about my training nowadays is that there is absolutely no motivation to train. Before the accident, I used to be motivated to go to the gym because I knew that my training was making me stronger and fitter – I was seeing results and continuously improving. When I would deadlift, for example, I would be able to lift about 5 kg more each week than I had the week before. So, I was motivated to get back in the gym and deadlift because I saw and felt myself get stronger. But since my accident I've been bicep curling the same 1 kg weight every single week for the past four years straight. So why do I do it? Because of discipline. I may not see any results next week, next month, or even next year, but one day, I will lift 1.5 kg and I will be thanking my current self that I kept on trying.

Some mornings, I leave the home gym and head to the rehab centre to practise on the walking machine or go to one of my bi-weekly physio sessions, which are two hours long. I hate every minute of my training, but I do it because I know it's good for me.

Because my ability to be physically healthy is compromised by my disability, I also take a very strict approach to my diet. I can't be as active as I used to be, so I need to watch what I eat a lot more than I used to. Once upon a time, I would smash a burger for lunch and a pizza for dinner and not think anything of it – because I was doing so much sport, I could pretty much get away with eating whatever I wanted. But I know that my diet plays a big factor in my overall health, which is why during the week I cut out most processed foods and all carbs. Don't get me wrong, I still love food, and restricting myself from eating certain things isn't something I like doing, but again it comes down to the discipline I apply to my daily life to ensure I'm maximising my time here and giving myself the best chance at reaching my potential. I'd love to sit down every night to a big bowl of penne arrabbiata with extra chilli, bacon and olives, have seconds, and then wash it down with some ice cream or a chocolate milkshake. But my desire to live a full and healthy life far outweighs even my desire for pasta. Sometimes you have to focus on long-term necessities instead of short-term pleasures. Again, it all comes down to discipline.

I also live and die by the calendar on my iPhone; I make my way through each day by completing task after task.

I schedule everything in the calendar – and I don't leave any time for wasting (or scrolling on TikTok). Every hour of my day between about 7 am and 10 pm is allocated to something worthwhile; every hour has a purpose. The only blank spots you'll ever find in my calendar are allocated travel time, for example, when I'm driving to or from work, or from work to physio. And that unallocated time is no more than thirty minutes a pop. I colour-code everything, too: green for uni, purple for medical appointments, yellow for meetings, red for public speaking, orange for training and what's left is blue. That's my favourite colour, because it's for my social life.

And I know it sounds a bit over the top, but it's the best way I've found to maximise my productivity day-to-day. It's also an active choice I make thanks to my newfound complicated relationship with time – knowing I have less of it than most people.

I've heard this saying that I love, which goes, 'If you give yourself 30 days to clean your home, it will take 30 days, but if you give yourself 3 hours to clean your home, it will take 3 hours', and that's how I feel when I'm using my calendar to manage my time. If I set aside a whole Saturday to finish one of my university assignments, it would take me the whole day to finish the assignment because I would have given myself enough time to procrastinate, get distracted, snack, chat to my parents, and so on. But if I allocate a two-hour block to just getting it done, I know I'll most likely finish it in 2 hours, leaving the rest of the day free for me to schedule other things.

Using a calendar the way I do also means I'm always hyper-aware of time. When I'm studying or working or doing whatever else I've allocated time to doing, I will get my phone, turn off auto-lock, prop it up against my laptop and open the calendar app so I can watch the red line slowly move through the allocated time slot like a countdown. I chase that red line from task to task in order to feel as accomplished and efficient with my time as I can, and that way I never let time slip away from me. My goal is to complete each task before the red line does – before the line moves through to the next task. I get a buzz every time I beat it. Now that I think about it, my life is like a race against the clock. It's me versus that red line. And this is why I've never understood people who say, 'I can't believe it's almost November', or 'Hasn't this week just flown by?' – I never feel that way because I'm so aware of where my time is going.

I make sure that every single night when my head hits the pillow that I'm completely exhausted; I need to be able to look back on the day and feel confident that I did everything I could have. By doing this every day, I hope that when I get to the end of my life I'll be able to do the same thing – I'll be able to look back on my life and honestly say to myself that I left nothing behind and that I did my *absolute best*.

Of course, I'm not a robot, I have had days where I chill out. But whenever I've had a rare relaxed day and slumped around not doing much, I've gone to bed that night feeling frustrated and annoyed knowing I didn't make the most of the day and, thinking about all the time I've wasted. Time I'll never get back.

Jim Rohn gave a lecture once saying that in life we have two choices; the pain of discipline or the pain of regret.

Yes, discipline is painful – declining that pizza, missing that party, sacrificing sleep, training your body hard. But I have realised that the pain of regret is way worse – feeling sick after bingeing on junk food; handing in a half-arsed assignment because you were hungover all of Sunday; sleeping in and falling behind with work; feeling weak because you've skipped training. And the most painful thing about regrets? They build up, and if you're not careful you'll get to the end of your life and regret never finding out what you could have done and become.

So, I choose the pain of discipline. My family isn't always supportive of the discipline I apply to my lifestyle. I think my parents wish I'd go easier on myself. They always tell me to sleep in for once, to get on the couch and relax, to have a break, or indulge in a serving of mashed potatoes. Even writing this book, Mum told me not to do it. She says I have too much on my plate. But my reply to her is always, 'I know, but what if it helps someone achieve their goals? What if it

I FIGHT, YOU FIGHT

makes someone a little happier? What if it saves someone's life? What if this message is passed on long after I die? What if writing a book is on the list that God has prepared for me?'

I also think my friends wonder what I'm doing it all for. Why I strive so hard and hardly ever just relax. *Have another beer, Alex – you barely drink anymore! Come to the club! Don't go home early again* . . . It's always tempting, but I know deep inside that when I get to the end and I look back on my life, it will all be worth it.

There's this saying I love, which is usually attributed to the artist Vincent Van Gough. It goes: 'Normality is a paved road; it's comfortable to walk, but no flowers grow on it.'

CHAPTER 17

WORKING IT ALL OUT

'The greatest use of life is to spend it for something that will outlast it.'
– William James

For the past couple of years, I have dared myself to try and answer the age-old question: what is the meaning of life?

Quite quickly, I thought I had it all figured out.

At first, the conclusion I came to was that the only thing that really matters in life is what you leave behind after you die. The universe is billions of years old and most of the things we do in our eighty or so years on Earth are completely immaterial to the rest of humankind – they leave no mark on history, and they have no impact on the future. The things we attain, the accomplishments we achieve, the money we make, the memories we create and the experiences we have along the way all die with us in the end. The role we played in this world might be remembered by our children, our grandchildren and possibly our great-grandchildren, but after this, our names and who we were will be completely forgotten forever. These things give us short term pleasure, satisfaction and fun while we're here, but they make no lasting difference to the world after we're gone.

My goal in life became to create something that would live on far longer than my years on the planet; something that could be passed down through future generations and that would make a positive impact on people after I'm gone. If I can achieve this, I told myself, I will be able to live forever, overcoming my fear of death and my fear of not reaching my potential.

As I pursued this idea, I started to engage in activities that I thought would help me leave a lasting – and ideally permanent – positive impact on the world. I identified things like public speaking, my social media channels, studying law and even writing this book. And as with everything I set my mind to, I started relentlessly pursuing these activities – almost going too far at times. I found myself deliberately not having fun or finding joy, because I knew it would mean nothing in the grand scheme of things, fading away into history like dust in the wind.

My obsession didn't escape the notice of the people around me. 'Alex, you need to have more fun in life – you need to relax and take a day off!' they said. At first, I shrugged off their concerns. 'Do you think Elon Musk or Steve Jobs took a day off? Do you think they achieved what they've achieved by worrying about work–life balance?' The answer, I was sure, was no. I was worried that if I took too much time off from pursuing my goals, I'd never get there – I'd never become the man I was destined to be. But it did get me thinking. What if there was more to life than leaving a legacy behind? What if that was just one piece of the puzzle?

After a few discussions with some important people in my life, including Jesse, Brooke, Benji and my parents, I realised that living a life wholly for the purpose of leaving behind a legacy was distracting me from the fun and joy life had to offer. So, I was back to square one: *What is the meaning of life?*

My little brother Benji noticed how hard I was racking my brain to find all the answers. It was April 2023 when he came to me with a short story he had written for school. I was surprised to see that I was the main character.

As a child, Alex had always been fascinated by the stories of great men who had left their mark on the world. He had dreamed of becoming one of them, of leaving a legacy that would endure long after he was gone. But as he grew older, he realised that time was not on his side. Every day that passed brought him one step closer to his inevitable end, and he knew that if he didn't act soon, his dreams would be lost in time like teardrops in rain.

Alex had always been a hard worker, and he had achieved a great deal of success in his career. But he knew that success was not enough. He wanted to do something that would make a lasting impact, something that would inspire future generations. He spent countless hours brainstorming ideas, but nothing seemed quite right.

One day, as he was walking through the park, he saw a young boy struggling to climb a tree. The boy was determined to reach the top, but he kept slipping and falling. Alex watched as the boy persisted, trying again and again, until he finally made it to the top.

As Alex watched the boy triumphantly look down at him from the treetop, he realised something. It wasn't about achieving something grand or monumental. It was about the small moments, the moments of perseverance and determination that made life worth living.

With this realisation, Alex set out to make the most of his time. He spent more time with his family and friends, and he took up new hobbies and interests that he had always been curious about. He found joy in the everyday moments, in the beauty of a sunset, or the sound of a bird chirping.

Alex's newfound appreciation for life didn't go unnoticed. His positivity and energy were infectious, and he inspired those around him to live their lives to the fullest. And when Alex passed away, he left behind a legacy that was not measured in dollars or accomplishments but in the memories and moments that he had shared with others.

In the end, Alex realised that time was not his enemy, but his greatest gift. It was a reminder to cherish every moment, to live with purpose, and to leave a positive impact on those around him. And in doing so, his moments in life would not be lost in time like teardrops in rain, but would endure for generations to come.

And that's when it hit me: I hadn't been wrong, I just hadn't been looking at the whole picture. And Benji's story had revealed it to me. The whole picture included reaching for the stars, sure, but it also included taking the time to enjoy the sunset along the way, taking pleasure in life's little moments, and sharing them with the people you love. I went back to the drawing board, and came up with the

I FIGHT, YOU FIGHT

true meaning of life – okay, not quite. But I did come up with five things to pursue to have a more meaningful time here on Earth:

1. **Create a legacy.** Make a positive difference; help people grow, help people become happy. Do something or create something that can be passed on from one generation to the next, so that it transcends the present, so that it lasts forever. This way, when you get to the end, although your body may be gone, you will never truly die.
2. **Achieve and maintain good health.** Never take it for granted, because without it, you're going to have a much harder time reaching your goals and getting what you want out of life.
3. **Love.** Love your family, your friends, your partner, your kids. There's no time limit on loving, and love can be its own kind of legacy.
4. **Have fun.** It's okay to enjoy yourself. Spending time with friends, eating good food, partying from time to time and travelling are all good for you. Stop and watch the sunset.
5. **Make money.** Money isn't everything, but it makes the other four goals a whole lot easier. Use it to change the world for the better, to pay for your gym membership and stay healthy, to take your friends out for dinner, to help your loved ones when they need it, to book your overseas adventures and buy bottles of Dom Perignon to celebrate your successes.

None of these things is enough on its own. What is the point of leaving a legacy behind if you don't enjoy life along the way? What use is good health if you don't do anything with it? Love is one of the best things in life, but love alone can't put food on the table or a roof over your head. Sure, having fun is important, but life shouldn't be an endless party with no purpose. And they say that money makes the world go round, but unless you spend it properly, it's ultimately worthless – you can't take it with you when you go!

I finally had the full picture.

I approach my life – I approach every day – with these five things in the back of my head. This way, not only will I be leaving my mark on the world long after I am gone, I will also have enjoyed and loved the journey of life.

~

So, I had a roadmap for life – now all I had to do was follow it. I'd gotten into the university course I wanted – business and law at the University of Technology Sydney – but now I actually had to get *onto* campus, get to class, and get to work. Just getting there would have meant arranging a support worker to come and pick me up and drop me off, and because my hand mobility is limited – I also wear these black fingerless gloves for wrist support – I couldn't even get my laptop out of my bag on my own. Meeting new people is awkward enough without having to ask randoms to fish around in my bag or explain to them why I'm wearing biker gloves!

But lucky for me, my mate Jesse — who I'd met in primary school — was doing the same degree, and we came up with a plan. We signed up for all the same classes so our schedules matched, and Jesse became my ride to uni as well as my study buddy in class. He went above and beyond, making my uni life a breeze, but he never made it seem like it was an effort or an inconvenience for him — we were just two mates, studying business and law and eating lunch together.

I don't know what I was really expecting from university, or what I had gotten myself into — I barely knew the difference between a barrister and a solicitor when I started! But I just charged on, into the unknown, and learned a lot.

I'm in my fourth year now and will graduate at the end of next year, in 2025. My favourite business subjects at uni are the accounting and finance ones, because I'm not bad at numbers and I like problem solving. I even managed to score a 99 in accounting, and you don't need to be good with numbers to know that 99 is pretty much as good as it gets! As for law, my favourite subjects so far have got to be commercial law and criminal law — we all love a Netflix true crime doco, but studying criminal law opens up a whole new world behind the scenes that I found fascinating. What I don't love is writing essays. I'd much rather do a test and apply my knowledge to answer problem scenarios than go on and on in a ten-page essay. Pretty ironic that I ended up writing a book, but life is full of surprises, isn't it?

I was in my second year at uni when I started thinking seriously about getting a part-time job. Most of my mates had jobs, but I hadn't had one since school. In fact, my first job in high school was as a drug dealer. No joke, I was literally delivering drugs to people – only not in the way you're probably thinking.

I was in Year 9 when my friend Zane hooked me up with a job at the local pharmacy where he worked. It was our job to deliver prescriptions to people in the area who couldn't make it to the pharmacy. After school on Fridays, my grandparents would pick me up and take me to work, where I'd jump on my pushbike, strap on my orange backpack full of drugs, and race through my delivery route. I must have been a pretty good drug mule, because the people I was delivering to – mostly sweet old ladies – often gave me tips. And tips were a big deal when you're only getting paid $9 an hour. Literally! On the other hand, maybe my work ethic could have been better – sometimes Zane and I would rip through our deliveries and finish early so we could take a break and ride down to Ogalo's to spend our tips on chips while we were still on the clock. I hope my old boss isn't reading this!

So, for various reasons, I wasn't sure how much my previous work experience was going to help me get a job. I knew I wanted to work in law, business or finance, but like many people my age I didn't know exactly what job I was looking for, or how to get it. But *unlike* most people my age, I also had quadriplegia to contend with. I knew it wasn't going to be easy. The opportunities weren't equal. Not all industries are accommodating.

I started applying for jobs online, but most of the time no one ever got back to me. When they did, it was usually a rejection. Multiple times, I got to the interview stage and I was told the business was happy to have me on board . . . And yet, the offer fell through. The companies ended up citing things like insurance and accessibility problems, or unsuitable technology as the reason they couldn't offer me a job. They all wanted me in their company, but couldn't actually figure out how to facilitate a quadriplegic in their company. The issue was my disability. Simple things like fire hazard regulations, for example, counted against me: I wouldn't be able to use a lift if there was a fire, but I wouldn't be able to use the fire stairs either. My disability stood in the way of me choosing a number of other career paths too – I could forget any sort of laborious or physical gig. It was an office job or bust.

Yes, I faced obstacles, but nothing worse than what I had been through and had come out the other side of already. I guess that's the beauty of such a traumatic life event like becoming a quadriplegic – everything that would usually be seen as difficult now seems easy in comparison. And, as I learned, things have a strange way of working out.

There's a Chinese proverb about a farmer that kind of sums up my struggle to get a job and more so, many of my struggles in life. It goes like this. One day, a farmer loses his horse, and so all of his neighbours come over and say to him, 'I'm sorry, that is terrible news.' To which the farmer replies: 'Well, maybe.' The next day, five horses come running onto his farm, and all of his neighbours declare, 'That's wonderful news!' To which the farm replies again, 'Well, maybe.' The next day, the farmer's son takes one of the horses out, and while riding he falls off it and breaks his leg. Again, all the farmer's neighbours come to him and say, 'I'm sorry to hear about your son, that is terrible news,' and he replies once more: 'Well, maybe.' A week later, some men from the military come up to the farm to take his son away to fight in a war, but because he is injured, they leave the farmer's son behind to live safely with his family.

The point of this proverb is that you never really know what the outcome of a situation is going to be. So, I decided to carry on, do my best, and see what's in store for me.

As you can imagine, I was feeling pretty fed up. But I didn't let it get to me – I figured there was no point wasting my energy on something I couldn't control. So, I decided to adapt to the circumstances. Despite the whole job-hunting exercise leaving me feeling quite demoralised, I took a step back and I said to myself: 'Okay, so I accept that employment is harder now, but what can I do about it?'

I FIGHT, YOU FIGHT

That path wasn't for me, so it was time to change tack; if I wasn't going to get employed by someone else, then I was going to *employ myself*. If I couldn't get a job in an office because of accessibility issues, then I'd look for one a little closer to home. And that's how Zeus Charters began – my private boat charter company.

My mum runs her own charter boat business called Eastcoast Sailing – renting out boats to people for events – and I figured I could help out on the back end, maybe get some business experience behind the scenes. One day, sitting at home and feeling defeated by the obstacles I was facing in getting an office job, I went to my parents with a business proposal: if they let me manage one of their boats, I would start my *own* charter business, run it, and share the profits with them. I must have made it sound like a pretty sweet deal, because they went for it. And I'm glad they did, because I've learned way more about business by starting my own one than I have in my whole business course at uni.

I had to work out pretty quickly how to use accounting software, manage human resources, do all the marketing, plan ahead and stick to a budget. In accepting defeat in one area, I had one of my biggest wins. I turned an obstacle into an opportunity. Zeus Charters has exposed me to all elements of business and it has taught me everything I now know about running a company. These days, the company offers packages for all kinds of events: corporate cruises, buck's and hens parties, birthdays and Christmas celebrations. We've got you sorted with BBQs and booze onboard for the perfect day out on the water. We even do whale watching, if that's your thing. And you'd better believe that the *Zeus* is wheelchair accessible.

Still, I guess I never entirely let go of the idea of working in an office and learning the ins and outs of how a bigger company operated, because when the opportunity finally presented itself, I jumped at it. I was in my second year of uni when I was asked to give a speech at my old school, Riverview, on mental health and the importance of speaking up as a man and asking for help. I spoke about my dream of working in law or finance one day, and funnily enough, there was someone in the audience who could help me make that dream a reality. One of the Riverview dads was the chief financial officer of a company, and apparently he liked the cut of my jib – to use a sailing metaphor – because he messaged my dad after hearing my speech and told him, 'If Alex wants a job in finance, I'll sort him out.' How about that? I'd spent so much time looking for jobs, and now one had found me.

I didn't get my hopes up, of course, because of all the job offers that had fallen through before. I knew that there was a chance that when my potential employer realised how complicated it could be for me to even access an office space, let alone work in one, he would have to back out. But this

I FIGHT, YOU FIGHT

time, I didn't need to worry – after an interview, we discussed logistics and before I knew it, I was officially hired.

Little did I know that getting the job was only the first of many workplace hurdles. When I rocked up to my first day on the job, I was feeling pretty nervous and vulnerable. There were the usual first day things to worry about: getting there on time, meeting new people and making awkward small talk, learning about my new role. But on top of this I also had to worry about a whole heap of other things: whether I could actually get into the building or not, who would help me if my wheelchair got stuck, what if I couldn't reach something, what if I couldn't physically use their laptops or software, how would I eat lunch – the sorts of things most people never have to think about.

But as it turned out, what *actually* happened was way, way worse than anything I could have imagined.

There I was, meeting my new manager in front of the whole office. I was wearing black linen pants, dress shoes and a button-up shirt, and I'm not going to lie – I was looking pretty schmick. As I was introduced to people, I actually started to think maybe I was going to be just fine – after learning to breathe and use my arms again, this job thing was going to be easy as.

And then disaster struck.

You see, when I'm at work or away from my family, friends and carers, I use what's called a 'night bag', which is just a nice way of saying a piss bag. Because I can't just get up and use the bathroom the same way I used to, and because I have no one with me who knows how to help me to the toilet, I connect my catheter to a thin tube that drains into the night bag, which sits in my backpack. It's pretty discreet . . . or at least it usually is. But on this day, as my manager stood beside me while showing me the company's income statement, somehow – and I'm not even sure exactly how – the tube disconnected from the bag and . . . well, you can guess how that went. Piss on the floor. Everywhere.

I was beyond embarrassed. Has anyone ever quit their job on day one? I'd be lying if I told you I didn't consider it. I was literally watching my brand-new manager cleaning my urine off the floor in front of the whole open-plan office, surrounded by at least thirty colleagues; how could I possibly face them all again the next day? And the day after that?

But it's in moments like this when you really have got to try and stop your mind from going to dark places. You've got to stop those negative thoughts from flowing in, because my God did they come flowing! *How can I ever have a normal life when I'm so hopeless?, Why would anyone employ me when all I am is a liability?, All I've ever done in life is try my best, but I still suck!,* and *Stuff this, I give up.* I wanted to just go home, curl up in my bed, lock the door and never leave. Life nearly had me beat.

I told myself to look at the big picture. Who will remember this when I'm eighty? Or in a hundred years from now? It's a

I FIGHT, YOU FIGHT

bit like the feeling you get when you look up at the stars and realise how tiny you truly are. In the grand scheme of things, a bit of piss on the floor doesn't matter. It's what you do after it's all cleaned up that counts. So, what did I do?

I assessed the situation by distinguishing between what I could and couldn't control, deciding to ignore the latter and just simply focus on what I *did* have control over. Not much at all, it turns out, but I did what I could. I lifted my catheter from hanging over my wheels to rest it on my leg so the continuously leaking piss would fall onto my pants rather than the floor. And then I did what anyone would do in this situation: I texted Mum and asked her to drive over and meet me outside. On top of all that, I couldn't actually get outside . . . I even had to ask my manager to open the door for me so I could make my escape!

After recuperating outside with Mum for about an hour, I had to face the hardest part of this whole event: re-entering the office. So what did I do? I called upon my comparison strategy. I imagined what would have happened if Mum wasn't available to come and help. In this situation, I would be spending the next six hours of the day with piss continually streaming down my legs, onto my cushion and into my shoes. In that scenario – the one I was imagining – I knew I would wish that I was in the situation I actually found myself in, with Mum there to turn my catheter off and stop the piss flowing. I would say to myself, 'If only Mum was here to reattach my night bag, I'd be so happy!' So, because Mum *was* there, and the piss was not spraying all over me for the next six hours, and I managed to dry my pants, I was grateful for that moment. I appreciated that moment and, believe it or not, was able to find joy in that moment.

So, after an hour of tossing up between calling it a day and going home, calling it off completely and resigning, or taking another hit, soldiering on and getting back in there, I went back in.

When things happen to us in life that we have no control over, we can sulk in the rain or we can dance in the rain but either way, it's going to rain. I choose to dance in the rain . . . or the piss.

CHAPTER 18
THE NOBLE WAY

'What you leave behind is not what is engraved in stone monuments, but what is woven into the lives of others.'
– Pericles

I've been asked this question a lot: 'If you could, would you go back to who you were before the accident?' And my answer to that is no. No way. Not mentally, anyway.

Since the accident, not much has changed, and yet everything has changed. I was always committed, competitive, motivated, focused and ambitious – but all of it was channelled towards footy. Now, I apply those same characteristics towards living a better and more fulfilled life. I'm dedicated to my work, I'm focused with my studies, I'm committed to my relationships, I'm ambitious with my own personal goals and I'm motivated to live the best life I can possibly live.

I sometimes find myself getting so focused on being the best human that I can be that I actually forget I'm a quad. So often, Mum sees me studying hard, or working hard, or overexerting myself to try to achieve this and that, and I know she gets concerned that I'm not 'happy'. She regularly asks me, 'Alex, are you happy?' and my reply is always: 'What is wrong? How could I possibly be unhappy?'

It's almost as though Mum sees my condition as more of a hindrance than I do, but I think I'm too busy chasing my purpose to be worried about my chair. My goal isn't just to be the best quadriplegic that I can be. And I don't have the same goals as the average person either. Yes, I have some of the same goals, like finding a wife, starting a family and having kids. But as I've said earlier, I also want to be great. I want to be extraordinary. I want to be a CEO. I want to be a Nelson Mandela. I want to be a Muhammad Ali. And more importantly, I also want to leave something behind that's bigger than myself.

I didn't know it at the time, but apparently I was sitting on some pretty profound learnings from my experience of becoming and living as a quadriplegic.

Early on in rehab days, Tess, my older and wiser big sister, told me that I was going to be a keynote speaker one day and that she could even see me writing a book. I laughed at her and said, 'Good joke – why would people want to hear from me?'

Every night in hospital, when my final visitor would say goodbye to me and go back home to get on with their own life, I would sit by myself and read over the comments and messages I received from my social media posts. Initially, I thought all of the likes and comments and messages were just acts of sympathy and support. But after a few months of reading more and more comments, I started to realise something. I realised that these people weren't just supporting me, I was actually supporting *them*. Unknowingly, I was somehow helping others. My actions and my mindset were inspiring others. I thought to myself, *Maybe, just maybe, Tess was right . . . 'What if' she was right?*

And that 'what if' was all I needed.

I immediately began to pursue this goal. The goal of sharing my perspective, philosophies, advice and strategies with others to hopefully help as many people as I possibly could.

After four years of consistent research, brainstorming, workshops and presentations, I finally established what I call The Noble Way. It's a four-stage method to approaching life that has helped me on my road to growing as a person, finding happiness and fulfilling my goals.

The four stages of The Noble Way are:

1. Master your mind
2. Pursue peace
3. Become resilient
4. Grow and achieve

Master your mind

When things don't go our way in life, naturally, our emotions immediately respond and take complete control of us. Our emotions go up, down, around, we get angry, then sad, then we grieve, and by the end of it, we are all worked up and plagued with uncontrollable negative thoughts. These disarrayed emotions and anxious thoughts or worries can blind us and stop us from thinking straight or seeing things clearly.

But, as I've said, it's not our circumstances in life that dictate how we feel; it's our judgements about our circumstances that do this. So, rather than focusing on trying to manage the circumstances we face, the focus should be on trying to manage our judgements *about* those circumstances.

When we can control our judgements, our minds become stronger than our emotions, and we can see past the emotions that cloud our decision-making. With a clearer mind, it's much easier to work out what we need to do in any given situation.

Remember when I was in the ICU? Not only had I lost control of my whole body, I had lost my whole purpose in life, my dreams of playing professional rugby. How could I possibly carry on when the only thing that I could do was roll my eyes? Well, I still had my mind, and as long as I had my mind, that's all I would ever need. Mastering your mind is the foundation of everything, I've learned, and one of the most powerful things you can do for yourself – it's about stepping outside of the situation, not letting those negative emotions and worries take over, and rationally focusing on what lies ahead.

To master the mind, you first have to believe that you have the power to do this. Once you're aware of just how powerful what you tell yourself is, you can assert control over what you think. You can decide how to respond to any circumstance. And once you have taken control of your thoughts and mastered your mind, you are one step closer to peace.

I FIGHT, YOU FIGHT

Pursue peace

What does peace mean? For me, peace is a state of serenity. A state of stability. A state of content. I have found that peace is the key to managing life when things get tough. It is the enabler of long-term happiness, the enabler of resilience and the enabler of growth. Peace, for me, is one of the most powerful feelings in the world.

Yet for something so important and so powerful, peace is a pretty rare thing. People often pursue happiness, and they rely on external things or situations to give them that happiness. But when we only pursue happiness – or specific things in life that we think will make us happy – we're setting ourselves up for failure. There will be sad days in even the happiest life, we won't always get what we want, and if all we ever do is hunt for happiness . . . well, we'll find ourselves pretty unprepared when things go wrong.

The pursuit of happiness is like a kite in the wind. The kite represents us and our emotions, and the wind represents the situations and circumstances we face. When the wind blows the right way, the kite goes the right way. But when the wind blows the wrong way, the kite goes the wrong way. And so, what happens on a day where the wind is wild? The kite comes crashing down and so will we.

But when we replace the pursuit of happiness with the pursuit of peace, we are able to go through life without its ups and downs knocking us off course and sending us into a downward spiral. We will be able to confront challenges and problems with a sense of clarity about what we need to do and how it needs to be done. The wind doesn't always blow the right way, but we will be able to steer through it.

I learned a lot about peace when I was cooped up indoors after I came home from rehab. Instead of raging against the situation I found myself in, I chose to pursue peace. Instead of focusing on all the things I was missing out on, I concentrated on all the good things I had in my life – my amazing family and friends, a roof over my head, the sunshine outside my window.

I still find myself searching for peace every day. No matter where I am in life, no matter how bad a situation is, I can always call upon it. I arrive at peace by finding gratitude during the good times, during mundane normality, and most importantly, in times of difficulty. I find this gratitude by comparing my situation to a situation that is worse off, which then always makes me realise how good my current situation actually is. And because we could always be worse off, no matter where we are in life, no matter how bad a situation is, we can always interpret our situation as a positive and find that state of peace.

And so, in achieving a state of peace, when the wind turns bad, we can continue to fly.

I FIGHT, YOU FIGHT

Become resilient

If you can master your mind and try to find a fundamental state of peace, you will have a strong foundation to become more resilient – which is a skill you're going to need if you want to achieve any substantial goal.

When the goal is hard and the road is long and you get to a point when you feel like giving up, it can be so easy to just call it quits. Do you know what I mean? Like when your email inbox is flooded and you feel like you are never going to get on top of it. Or when all your exams are at the same time and you're getting really stressed out. Or when work is getting too busy and you feel like you have no time for your family or personal life. Or when you keep trialling for that sports team but you just can't quite make it. It's these moments in life where true, relentless resilience is needed.

It doesn't matter how many times you get knocked down, all that matters is that you get back up. Having resilience means not letting those knockbacks push you off your path and get you down – it means trying again, and again, and again, and again until you succeed.

The best way I have found to remain resilient is to break down my goals into more manageable tasks. Because, guess what? Small knockbacks are easier to bounce back from than big ones, and small tasks are easier to achieve than big ones, too. I didn't go from the ICU to suddenly trying to stand up. It all started with seeing the time on the clock for the first time, remember? Then it was learning to breathe on my own again. Then it was learning how to talk again, then to drink, eat, move, live. Then it was day after day in the gym, doing the same things over and over, barely seeing any success or progress. But with this resilience, day in and day out, week in and week out, year in and year out, I am now able to eat by myself, go to work, get to bed without a ceiling hoist and I can even do a 20 kg squat.

If you're always looking far off into the distance at some seemingly impossible goal, it's easy to get frustrated when you fail to get there in one go, and just quit trying altogether. But if you look down at the ground beneath you and focus on the steps you need to take to reach your goal, all you ever have to do is take one more step. A marathon runner can't jump to the finish line, and neither can you. You've got to move towards your goals one step at a time, and have enough resilience to stay on track and bounce back from any obstacle on the road.

Grow and achieve

Taking control over your thoughts and emotions, pursuing peace and becoming more resilient are the foundations that have allowed me to grow as a person and achieve goals in my life. But I hope that these lessons I've learned the hard way will also help you to reach your own goals in life – whether your goal is to make that sports team, to get that job, to create a beautiful family, to make a positive change in the world, to reach your potential, or simply to be happy.

In my own life, I've had a lot of highs and lows, but I've also reached many of my goals. Not only have I gone from being pinned to a bed unable to breathe to squatting 20 kg, I also managed to graduate Year 12 after being in hospital and missing nearly a year of school. I received a 96.7 ATAR, came third in New South Wales for PDHPE, received a gold certificate for application to studies and was awarded the 'Insignis' medal – Riverview's most prestigious award. I managed to get into a business and law degree at university, where I've received high distinctions in various subjects. I've entered the workforce and been employed in a finance company and a law firm, and I've even started up my own boat charter company. I have received the 'Ryde Young Citizen of the Year' award. I've also travelled the world, ridden on camels, sailed across the Heads of Sydney Harbour in a tiny sail boat, gone jet skiing, snorkelling, surfing and skydiving. I've presented in front of hundreds of thousands of people all over Australia, reached millions of viewers on my TikTok, and shared my message with thirty thousand of my followers and beyond on Instagram. I have also been lucky enough to have the opportunity to spread my message on countless podcasts, in magazines and in four documentary series. I've even been in a movie! And I am now, apparently, an author.

I've been able to achieve some pretty cool things in my life. And I couldn't have done it all on my own – I have had truly incredible help and support from the people around me, and I know how lucky I am. But all the help in the world wouldn't have been enough on its own. That's where The Noble Way fits in.

Following the advice I set out for myself in The Noble Way has helped me grow and achieve so much – and it applies to all goals in life; big and small. But, if you're like me and you not only want to achieve goals, but discover just how far you can go in life, the question remains – how do we maximise our growth and achievements? Well, remember those three big life lessons I mentioned earlier? Those have been the key principles that have helped me maximise my growth and achievements (so far, anyway): accept what you can't control, embrace discomfort and vulnerability, and be disciplined.

Accept what you can't control

Accepting what we can't control prevents us from getting stuck in the mud of our past and present adversities, allowing us to continue on our journey into the future and towards our goals. We won't successfully complete the waterslide if we don't let go of the handlebar behind us. An aeroplane won't take off if it holds onto the runway behind it. And you can't drive your car looking in the rearview mirror. Accept what you can't control, focus on what you can, and continuously strive forward.

I FIGHT, YOU FIGHT

Embrace discomfort and vulnerability
The greatest goals and accomplishments in life aren't usually things we can just reach out and grab from where we're sitting comfortably. The bigger the goal, the more difficult it is to get there and the more out of reach it can seem. So, instead of playing the game of life in our comfort zones and sitting around waiting for our dreams to fall into our laps, we have to *grow towards them*. And the only way to grow is to push ourselves out of that comfort zone, get uncomfortable, embrace the feeling of being vulnerable and constantly ask the question: *What if*? No extraordinary person lived an easy and comfortable life. The most beautiful views are often at the top of the steepest and scariest trails.

Be disciplined
On the road to achieving your dreams, it's also going to get tough. In fact, at times, it's going to be absolutely excruciating. Some days, training or working is going to be the last thing that you feel like doing. But that is what it takes. And that is why discipline is needed . Discipline is sacrificing something that you want right now for something better later on. Sacrificing your current self to help your future self. Sacrificing short-term desires for long-term goals. But I tell you what, your future self will be so glad you did it — the feeling of accomplishing those goals makes it all worth

it in the end. Often, the more painful the process, the greater the achievement and the more accomplished you will feel.

~

We all have the ability to reach our potential in life, but very few of us ever actually get there. This is because the standards and expectations we set around what we can do and what we can achieve is often lower than what we are truly capable of achieving. We are all capable of achieving so much more than we think we can. We are all capable of becoming so much better than we are. The only things that stop us from reaching our full potential in life are our own choices: our choice to feel sorry for ourselves and give in to grief, our choice to seek comfort instead of growth, our choice of pleasure instead of discipline, and our choice to never truly go searching for our full potential.

So, to break down these limitations and truly achieve our potential, we must accept what we can't control, embrace discomfort and vulnerability, be disciplined and be courageous enough to explore what our full potential really is. This way, we will become who we are capable of becoming. This way, when we come to the end of our lives, we won't be filled with the regret of knowing we could have done more with the time we had – we will be filled with the satisfaction of knowing we couldn't have done any better.

I FIGHT, YOU FIGHT

I wrote this short piece in my journal which I think sums up my approach to life and The Noble Way pretty well.

Reflecting on trauma imprisons your soul. Addictions and desires enslave your soul. Comfort kills your soul. Find peace by finding gratitude throughout difficulties, become disciplined and embrace vulnerability and your soul will become free. Become a free soul and you will find happiness, growth and fulfillment.

This book might make it seem like my life is easy now, like I have it all figured out, like everything is perfect. But the truth is, it's far from it. My journey has been hard – it still is, and it always will be. I have a long and tough road ahead of me; I still face challenges every day of my life, I still find myself in completely unfair situations and I still have chronic issues that never leave my side. But as long as I can call upon The Noble Way, I know I can get through anything.

The Noble Way is something I came up with because it worked for me. I realised I needed to share it with the world when I started receiving feedback from people of different walks of life; not just people who have been through a traumatic accident or those living with a disability, but CEOs, professional athletes, mothers, fathers, primary school kids, teenagers, the list goes on. And here is what just a few of them had to say:

'Thank you for inspiring me to keep fighting . . . so many times I have thought of giving up because it's too hard but then I listen to you and you motivate me to keep on going. You're the reason I am still going on with my life. So from me and any everyone you've inspired, thank you so much.'

'With all my mental health issues, I struggle to live my life every day. I struggle getting out of bed, I struggle to leave my house, I struggle to eat and when I came across your videos, it made me realise that sometimes life can hit you so hard but we need to get back up and I'm going to continue to fight my battles and demons and stay strong! So I want to say thank you so much for everything honestly.'

'Thank you for sharing your mindset and outlook on life, you are inspiring more people than you know.'

'I have learnt so much from you and I have changed the way I approach my life. I often give advice to my family and kids, advice that I have learnt from you.'

'Your words are so helpful for me and my kids, you will make changes in a lot of people's perspectives for the better.'

'On tough days, I come to your page. Within minutes I'm powered up once again. Thank you for helping us all with your incredible wisdom. You are spreading a wonderful message and are making the world a better place.'

I FIGHT, YOU FIGHT

It's comments like these that get me out of bed in the morning and give me purpose. I will read them on my deathbed one day and know that, although my body will be gone, I will continue to live on through the message I leave behind.

I hope to spend the rest of my life sharing The Noble Way with people, schools, companies, sports teams and organisations from around the world and inspiring them to not give up, to overcome challenges, to find happiness, to achieve their goals and to reach their full potential. And now I've shared it with you in the hopes that something you read here sticks with you. I hope there's something in this book that you can apply in your own life, whatever road you find yourself on. But more than anything, I hope that the lessons I've learned can help you achieve the goals you are pursuing and become the best person you can possibly be. If I fight, you can fight too.

ACKNOWLEDGEMENTS

Throughout my journey, I have been incredibly fortunate to receive an immeasurable amount of support – from my closest family and friends, from organisations, institutions and businesses, and from people I don't even know. Despite my deep appreciation for all of this, I feel like I have never had a proper chance to thank everyone for what they have done for me. So, I'm going to take the opportunity now.

Firstly, I want to thank the team at Simon & Schuster Australia for making this book come to life. I thank my marketing and publicity team, specifically Jade and Kelly. I am particularly grateful to Erin and Lizzie for helping me write this book, for putting up with my perfectionism and for constantly reminding me that it's not a speech, it's a book! Lastly, I am deeply appreciative of Emma, my publisher, who first believed in me and gave me this opportunity. Thank you for your guidance and support on this new adventure of mine.

I extend my thanks to all of the schools, groups, teams, organisations, institutions, businesses, charities and entities that supported me in countless ways during my recovery journey. You all empowered me to get back up when I fell, enabled me to carry on and inspired me to fight. I thank all of the sporting teams for the amazing charity events and for welcoming me back into the rugby community. I also acknowledge the incredible support from companies who have helped me to become more independent, to adapt my home and to reengage with society.

I send my thanks to the numerous schools who have also supported me in all sorts of ways and in particular, I want to thank my school – St Ignatius College, Riverview. The Riverview community not only dedicated itself to helping me adapt and overcome the many barriers that I faced when returning to school, it also taught me many of the principles I live my life by. For the values you've instilled in me and for getting back to school and into university when I thought my future was ruined, I am forever grateful.

I am also especially grateful to every single person who participated in the Alex Noble Gala night on 23 February 2020. I specifically thank the organisers – Julie, Caroline, Laurie and their band of sub-committees – for coordinating the whole event and making it one of the most special nights of my life. I'll never be able to thank you enough.

I also wanted to give a huge thank you to everyone that has played a role in my physical training and rehab programs.

I FIGHT, YOU FIGHT

Your dedicated guidance and assistance throughout each and every one of my training sessions has made me stronger and more independent than I ever thought possible. I'd like to thank my primary physio Adrian who has trained with me for four hours a week, every week, for the past five years – your skills, advice and commitment to help me achieve my best have optimised my recovery and enhanced my quality of life. I must also thank Ryde Royal Rehab, my home for eight months. The physios, nurses, therapists, accommodation, facilities and programs at Ryde were incredible – the team supported my family and I through the toughest period of our lives and helped me get back to where I belong: at home with my family.

I am so grateful to all of my carers who help me every day to do all of the things that I cannot. Without you, I would not have been able to achieve what I have, and I wouldn't be doing any of the things I'm doing today, literally. Thank you, not only for your help, but for making the time we spend together enjoyable, even when the routines get tedious and frustrating. I appreciate all of the great moments we've had together, and I do not consider you as carers – I consider you my friends.

A massive thank you to Kylie Gillies, who has been one of my biggest supporters since day one. You have used your skills, compassion and care in an extraordinary way to continuously support me and raise awareness of spinal cord injuries. There is no one better suited to introducing my book to the world, and I thank you for this and for everything.

To Harrison, Ash, Tye and Tess – my fellow roommates at rehab – I could not have asked for a better crew to be by my side through the most traumatic period of my life. We lifted each other up whenever one of us was down, we shared ideas and insights with each other while we learned to live a whole new life, and we found a way to have fun along the way.

To Tess, you deserve a paragraph of your own. Words cannot express how thankful I am for all of the support you have given me and the sacrifices you have made for me since I first met you in hospital. Simply out of the goodness of your own heart, you have dedicated so much of your time and effort into helping me spread my message and fulfil my purpose in life. You believed in me when I didn't, and you never gave up on me. Your commitment is the reason I'm doing what I'm doing today – without you there would be no keynote presentations, there would be no book, and I may never have found my purpose. For everything, I thank you.

My final thanks go to those that are most important to me: my family and friends.

To my friends, I remember when I first got injured and I woke up four days later to find that many of you had messaged me the same quote: 'God gives his toughest battles to his strongest soldiers'. You may not have realised it at the time, but each of you is one of those soldiers. When I went headfirst into battle, you came right along with me and you never left my side. When I got knocked down, you picked me right back up. When I was about to give up, you pushed me forward. Every day in hospital and rehab you were there supporting me; every physio and OT session, every lunch break and every visiting hour, you were there. Thank you for fighting this battle alongside me because without you, I would have lost.

I must give a special mention to a few of my friends who I no longer consider friends, but brothers. To the 211 boys – Jayden, Dylan, Connor, Zane and Jayme – thank you for being my best mates for the past eighteen years. I could not have asked for a better group of guys to share my childhood with and the rest of my life with. From boogie boarding in the sewer of Morrison Bay Park to celebrating birthdays in Ibiza and Greece, the memories we have made have shaped me and the memories we are yet to create excite me. For everything you have done, for everything we have done together, and for everything we are yet to do, I thank you and I love you. And finally, to Brooke – you are one of the best things that has ever happened to me, and I hope you know what you mean to me and how much I appreciate you.

My family, where do I start? I am particularly grateful to Nanna, who is the most resilient and selfless person I know.

The help and love you give to me and the family blows my mind and I'm so lucky to have you. I also thank Nanna, Pa and Uncle Brian, for spending just about every day with me in hospital so that I was never alone, and for meal deliveries that meant I never had to eat the hospital food. As for my mum, my dad, and my brothers: words will never be able to express how grateful and thankful I am to have you. For the past five and a half years, every single morning when I wake up, and every single night before I go to sleep, I have thanked God that I have you in my life. You have sacrificed so much of your own lives to make sure that I can live mine as part of this amazing family. I can't thank you enough for helping me with the constant daily challenges I face – especially those challenges that no one else sees. Your unwavering love, strength and support are the reason I'm still carrying on today. You have been right by my side at the beginning of my life, at the lowest points of my life, at the highest points of my life, and I know you will still be right by my side at the end of my life. For all of the amazing memories we have created, the lessons you have taught me, and the love you have given me, I thank you. I truly could not have asked for a better family to be by my side, living this life the Noble way. I love you so much.

ABOUT THE AUTHOR

Alex Noble was a sixteen-year-old rugby star with a promising sporting career ahead of him when an on-field accident landed him in a four-day coma in the ICU. Diagnosed with C4 quadriplegia, Alex was not expected to have any movement from the chest down.

Defying the odds, Alex's mental strength and resilience have seen him make incredible gains – from standing with minimal assistance to walking with the aid of an exoskeleton. At twenty-one, he now has a successful public speaking career, and between intensive weekly training regimes and university classes, he also works in a law firm, travels the world and runs his own boat charter business. Alex's achievements, perspective and message have inspired thousands to strive for their own goals and become happier.

Follow Alex on Instagram @ifightyoufight, or visit his website at www.alexnoble.com.au